Woman Without Background Music

Woman Without Background Music

Delia Domínguez

Translated by
Roberta Gordenstein with Marjorie Agosín

Edited by
Marjorie Agosín

The Secret Weavers Series, Volume 20

WHITE PINE PRESS / BUFFALO, NEW YORK

Publication of this book was made possible, in part, with public funds from the
New York State Council on the Arts, a State Agency, and by an award from the
National Endoment for he Arts, which believes that a great nation deserves great
art.

NATIONAL
ENDOWMENT
FOR THE ARTS

Printed and bound in the United States of America.

First Edition

Cover image by Nana Domínguez.

Library of Congress Control Number: 2005929020

10-digit ISBN: 1-893996-40-9
13-digit ISBN: 9781893996403

Published by
White Pine Press
P.O. Box 236
Buffalo, New York 14201
www.whitepine.org

Contents

from *Pido Que Vuelva Mi Ángel*
I Ask My Angel to Return (1982)

from *La Gallina Castellana* / *The Spanish Hen* (1995)

from *Neruda Sin Mesa De Tres Patas*
Neruda Without a Crystal Ball (1999)

from *Huevos Revueltos* / *Scrambled Eggs* (2000)

from *Clavo de Olor* / *Scent of Clove*

Woman Without Background Music

Introduction to Delia Domínguez

Beyond the mists where memory disguises and sometimes illuminates dreams, the poetry of Delia Domínguez emanates from the deep vastness of the land: her language is her homeland. In the zones of southern Chile, alongside ferns of astonishing verdure, fresh- and salt-water lakes, majestic and capricious volcanoes, Delia Domínguez is poetry and creates poetry. It would be impossible to separate her from those roots, those environments where her alphabet forged alliances with a nature that presages all events and signs.

In the 40th parallel, as she identifies her location on her farm in Tacamó, eight kilometers from the city of Osorno, Delia Domínguez plays with words and silence, with the rhythm of birds that announce the arrival of the rains, guests or the perpetual sounds of death. From this seat of honor that fabulates mythology and poetry, Delia Domínguez constructs her language based on experiences of life that surround her: the madwoman of the village who predicts the truth with hair-raising clarity:

Woman Without Background Music

You're there
burdened with the silence of life
or with the silence of death,

and your valor resembles wind
that never ceases, and mortar
from the wall splits your cheeks,
and other things
also split your cheeks:
      the weight of salt
      what's swallowed and what passes
      from rib to rib,
because Our Father who art in heaven
sometimes
topples heaven into our faces
and a woman can wind up leaning back at night
with a lightning bolt between her arms.

But you know what to do when your heart's
      breaking, and so you swear without blinking,
without bowing your head
and the footprints of everything you loved
keep turning into doves
like the circles of mourning under your eyes,
where tears
never stayed forever.

You're there
with all your love in your knees
and your strength flutters its wings
above the smoke from bonfires in the camps,
where the last lanterns must be extinguished
and only the heart rides horseback in the shadows.

And you're always vigilant
because heaven has fallen on you
at least fifty times without background music,
and it's also fallen on me
like a hand grenade

to the deepest sigh of despair,
and that was the coming-of-age, they said,
when the time came to respond
never withdrawing faced with a sharp-edged sign of
        time that pierced the dreams
where we slowly gathered hope.

You're there,
split in two above the earth
run through by children
by scars stitched
like Indian tents
that awaited dawn in the countryside.

You're there, without background music,
because you don't need background music,
simply your blue blouse
freedom of movement
and the ground you walk on.

Or the desperately poor woman whose courage goes beyond any known language. There are also the ancestors who accompany her to emphasize her origin again and again. The necessity for naming one's ancestors and being named. Great-grandparents, grandparents, and parents surround this poetry and this environment which is at the same time familiar and intimate but equally the fabulator of other stories that unite to construct one of the most daring, innovative and brilliant voices of contemporary Latin American poetry.

I have often wished to describe, to define, perhaps to explain, to myself and to English-speaking readers, the power this poetry exerts on its readers and on generations of Chilean poets who are her most loyal followers, especially those who live in southern Chile. One must respond to this wish with several ideas, among them the vitality of the colloquial and at the same time, lyrical, identity this poetry arouses. Like Czeslaw Milosz, the Polish Nobel Laureate, or lines by Russian poet Anna Akhmatova that recreate her century, Delia Domínguez has made her country her language. The orality of this poetry is the orality of the West: it recounts stories anchored to the root of the fable but at the same time to the root of what moves us as human beings.

> In the south
> the dead aren't buried,
> they dissolve in the mist.
> ("Question of Life or Death")

It is also an orality in constant search of collective social justice, a conscious call to the reality experienced not only by the American continent but also by the entire planet in the twenty-first century, a planet as impoverished and defrauded as "The Children of the Rain."

> The children of the rain ascend and descend along
> the silvery seam the moon stitches in the mountains.

> The children of the rain are the grandchildren
> of a mestiza grandmother who stayed behind to die
> in houses built of larch trees that bordered the lake.
> the children know how to tramp through the swamps like
> blind horses, but at the slightest misstep
> they turn into arrows
>   or ghostly dwarves.

These verses can be read as stories of otherness, of alternates, as well as of consciousness sublimated to a lyric poetry unforgettable for the spare elegance of its images, for a rhythm which at times is revealed to us like a prayer, an ancestral oration predating language but not poetry which is a visceral chant, a wild and vagabond root. In all these words we can find what defines the voice of Delia Domínguez, who with verbal economy and dexterity of thought creates an even more profound voice with the poetic canon of the twentieth century. For example, there are elements in the voice of Delia Domínguez that harmonize with the *Duino Elegies* by Rainer Maria Rilke, elegies that appear to have been dictated by the angels, by the spirits of the forests where Delia Domínguez practices her craft, her attire of a woodland woman always attached to an apprenticeship of the winds, the music of ancestors and beloved voices, as in the eulogy to Mahler at the ends of the earth:

Mahler Space

Here in the southernmost part of the world,
where the silence of the living
forms a body with the silence
of the dead
and everything is an empty cathedral nave,
a prayer,
in the symphonic percussion of the wind,

here in the south
Mahler passes through me. Carl Gustav Mahler, in
the four cardinal directions
where space is a breath from
antarctic tongues
a redeeming cold, free like a condor
on high.

In the poetic empire of Delia Domínguez, her sovereignty is vast and is linked to the crossbreeding of her native land as well as that of a Europe that she, by means of memory and the invention of memories of others, makes her own, just as Mahler dialogues with Sibelius. She unites the vision of Selma Lagerloff with Gabriela Mistral's American landscape and Pablo Neruda's devotion to the objects of an ever-changing nature.

Delia Domínguez writes a poetry of hybrid roots, as profoundly American as she is, defining herself through her work or in her inaugural discourse on becoming a member of the Chilean Academy of Language, but this crossbreeding is also the inheritance of other languages, the history of other histories, that she herself incorporates in her poetic territory, in the music of her senses.

The German colonizers who reached the south of Chile, as well as those from Nordic lands, her great-grandparents who, from the port of Hamburg, dared to reach the Americas, also form part of the cosmo-vision of Delia Domínguez. Her Americanism has absolutely nothing to do with a facile magical realism but rather with a concept of hybrid crossbreeding that knows how to create mosaics, historical voices that dialogue between past and present, between the tenderness of Rilke and the Americanism of Mistral. Among these voices is that of Delia Domínguez, enigmatically her own yet different from other poets of her environment and her generation. Although she is heir to a European-American vision of poetry, I dare say that her voice is absolutely unique, a voice one learns to read the way one moves deeply into a polyphony of voices or an alchemy of perfect harmony where a tapestry of images, sounds, and the avatar of conscience profiles a poetry that intoxicates, seduces and captivates the senses, like the secrets of the Cabala.

Her work is vast, consistent with an imaginary that continues polishing, braiding, purifying, one might say through her great labor as a poet, because it is a labor of every day and every night. Delia's poetry is solid, consistent with a vision of the world in which interiority and exteriority conjure the magic of her universe. And I say magic because all these poems obey the history of a rhythm, the insinuation of a sign, but most importantly, they obey her.

Many of the poems by Delia Domínguez assume an autobiographical voice, a self-portrait and the presence of an "I" that recounts and weaves her story:

> I'm like the animals...
> I sense misfortune in the air
> And I don't sleep on shifting sands

In other poems of introspection and her own story, the self-portrait turns into a challenge as in the poem, "Strike of Lowered Arms," where she describes herself with transparent, almost brutal, honesty:

> Today I refuse to feel vulnerable.
> Today I won't write. I cover my Achilles heel
> and all heels with a plaster cast.
>
> I'm not in the mood for great deeds. Today I refuse to
>   write.
> I declare myself on strike ladies and gentlemen.

The theme of the "I" facing a circumstance that is at the same time a space of enunciation, land and memory, becomes more elaborate with a precision purified throughout the trajectory of her poetry.

But in her unpublished manuscript, *Clavo de olor*, that appears here for the first time, the self-portrait defines and inscribes itself in a poetry of overwhelming strength:

> I'm the one death resuscitates at times
> and I divine the notebooks of a future
> that's an invention of the dead and buried past
>
> I'm the one who lives in the southern swamps
> who has no need of bodyguards
> against the splinters that suddenly burst the
> planetary system

of heavenly order
to reclaim the power of God
against the power of man.

From this trajectory of self-portraits, a unique thread stands out that borders on transparency, that is inscribed in a particular mythology surrounded by the avatars of mist, the currents of air, the omens of rain and an astral chart that corresponds to an environment, a feudal American territory at the southern tip of the world, a house built of wood inhabited by ancestors who roam through its rooms defying the laws of life and death. This is a poetry that demands a space for itself and urgently demands to exist, forged between the exterior limits of nature and the interior limits of the soul.

And here I am, seated between Comala and Tacamó,
    shoring up
border stars that aren't borders,
because at the end of the world
there are no limits, no separation of goods.
It's all Patagonia and it makes no difference
that earth is above and heaven below.

It is this permanence that permits the articulation of an intimate and fragile discourse facing a vulnerability of the poet who lives surrounded by an intense and profound loneliness, the loneliness of the being facing God, facing the language and history she must narrate.

The poem, "I'll Be Here When the Rains Return," perhaps represents the lyrical vision of Delia Domínguez from the very beginnings up to her most recent collection of poetry, *Clavo de olor:*

I'll be here when the rains return
when the house is a realm silent
as an old woman's memory

An old woman's memory is the memory that reclaims the regions of past and present, the presence of the dead and the living and in particular, the invisible women sunken in an oblivion of origin, like the crazy women of the town or the Vicky Baezes who pass unnoticed through the world but are seen and loved by the redeeming eye of the poet who assures that she is constantly remembered.

In this first English translation of her work, I wish for the audience to approach her poetry as her environment, to understand the significance of Chile, with its river salmon, its rural mischieviousness, its herbal teas, to become familiar with the work of a daring, prevailing poet amazed by her own geography, a poet related to the best of the culture and history of the Americas. In her we find echoes of Walt Whitman and Pablo Neruda, enigmas of place, like the mysterious Emily Dickinson of Amherst, signs of Juan Rulfo's territory of death, as well as the vision of a woman fragmented and alone but never defeated, like those in the works of Gabriela Mistral. Besides this familiar relationship with the continent, Delia Domínguez is also heir to Rilke, Cernuda and Lagerloff, and the musicians Bach, Brahms, Mahler and Sibelius to whom she listens repeatedly in her chair, carried from Vienna by the colonists to the southern tip of the world, to the southernmost point of the planet that Delia Domínguez names and baptizes, a territory she enumerates to assure its permanence in the impermanence of a century devoid of faith.

The poetry of Delia Domínguez can also be linked to a poetry that is essentially Catholic but not ritualistic in its conception of God. Since this is a poetry of conscience and humility facing the fragility of the human being, facing her own faith, Domínguez establishes a dialogue with faith and with the history of her faith. It is a poetry of socio-political protest, facing men, but more than anything, facing herself.

These poems were selected after almost twenty years of reading and study. They were also approved by the author herself in the Chilean summer of 2003 when I visited Delia Domínguez in her home in Osorno and understood that she is one with the place and with her verse. This is only a sample of a poetry of extraordinary value that deserves to be known in the Americas.

I remember her, I imagine her and sense her in Tacamó with her black lead pencil that she says writes by itself, because she writes by hand, foreign to the capricious laws of technology. She sits down in the afternoons to decipher the signs of the north or south wind and the music of birds she recognizes by both their scientific and common names. I look at her and I imagine her from childhood, intuiting the secret symbology of objects and the mystery of the alphabet and poetry.

In Tacamó I learned to recognize each one of her poems, gestures of love opposed to oblivion, prayers and orations for God and man. I learned that rain and damp woods surround her and demand that she be the voice that retells their secrets about the fire that melodiously obliges us to imagine forms. And so between fable and myth, American crossbreeding and the history of a Europe that still prevails in family portraits, Delia Domínguez is without doubt a poet of America, a poet of all times, but especially, her own descendent, joined to the ritual of an atavistic space, a space that opens the mansions to the most intimate and purified language, that of true poetry... a sacred and human language. Delia lives in the memory of everyday Osorno. Her poetry is always a wave, a constant return, a voice I found on the local radio station as I was leaving Osorno. In this environment where psalms blend with the voice of women of the countryside, Delia Domínguez writes stories of love with her black lead pencil.

> When a child is born
> —your own or another's—
> his great accomplishment of being born
> belongs to all of us.
> ("Community Of Love")

—Marjorie Agosín
Wellesley College

Introducción a las lluvias de Delia Domínguez

Las regiones frías del sur de Chile, letárgicas, hipnóticas, obligan a una expresión ensimismada: del balbuceo verde del follaje cuelgan versos llovidos y lluviosos, ramales de indecisa claridad y humedad.

Destacándose en la brumosa latitud brotan de pronto esquirlas encendidas por el volcán, hexágonos y triángulos de la nieve superior, rachas de viento que estallan como explosiones.

Entre estos síntomas de interrupción y rebelíon se sitúa el lenguaje de Delia Domínguez. Ignora el sopor evaporado que flota sobre los empapados pastizales: su comunicación es aguda como herramienta, recta y sonora.

La humanidad no fue aplastada por la noche ni la lluvia: toca la lana, la luna, el agua, la harina, los cuerpos, la ropa y el amor, sin vegetalizarse, sin convertirse en enredadera.

Es grande, pues, su delicado canto humano, sobreviviente victorioso de los grandes espacios que ordenan aquel silencio. Sus composiciones como Tos de perro, Los cómplices, y muchísimas otras de sus líneas nos imponen una alegría silvestre, la salud de una estirpe campesina y su desacomodo arterial hacia las indígenas ciudades. Es así su apostura de enérgica paloma de los montes.

Compréndase que por naturaleza, por formación ecológica, la poesía de Delia Domínguez, osornina de los bosques de Osorno,

es atrevida y descalza: sabe caminar sin miedo entre espinas y gui-
jarros, vadear torrentes, enlazar animales, unirse al coro de las aves
australes sin someterse al tremendo poderío natural para conversar
con tristeza o con amor con todos los objetos y los seres.

Mi amiga silvestre, criada entre los avellanos y los helechos
antárticos domina la relación humana con la ternura que adquirió
aprendiendo y defendiéndose de la soledad.

Yo quiero mucho a Delia Domínguez, y quiero que la quieran,
que la deseen, que se alimenten de las sustancias infinitamente fra-
gantes que nos trae desde tan lejos.

¿No es ése el destino del pan y de la poesía?

—Pablo Neruda
Isla Negra, Chile,
1973

Prologue to the book, *El sol mira para atrás,* written in Isla Negra one month
before his death.

Introduction to the Rains
of Delia Domínguez

The frigid regions of southern Chile, lethargic, hypnotic, demand an expression wrapped up in itself: from the green stammering of the foliage hang wet and watery verses, branches of undecided clarity and humidity.

Conspicuous in the misty latitude, splinters ignited by the volcano suddenly spring forth, hexagons and triangles from the snow above, gusts of wind that burst like explosions.

Within these symptoms of interruption and rebellion lies the language of Delia Domínguez.

It does not know the evaporated lethargy that floats above the drenched pasturelands: her communication is sharp as a tool, direct and sonorous. Humanity was not crushed by the night or the rain: it touches wool, the moon, water, flour, bodies, clothing and love, without taking root, without being converted into a climbing vine.

So her delicate human song is great, a victorious survivor of the immense spaces that command that silence. Her compositions such as "Barking Cough," "Accomplices," and so many of her other lines impose upon us a wild joy, the health of a country people, and her arterial discomfort towards the unworthy cities. Thus her bearing of an energetic mountain-dwelling bird.

Understand that by nature, by ecological formation, the poetry of Delia Domínguez, native of Osorno, from the woods of Osorno, is daring and barefoot, knowing how to walk fearlessly among thorns and pebbles, ford torrents, lasso animals, join the chorus of austral birds without submitting to the tremendous power of nature in order to converse sadly or lovingly with all objects and beings. My uncivilized friend, raised among hazelnut trees and antarctic ferns, masters the human relationship with the tenderness she acquired learning about, and defending herself from, loneliness.

I love Delia Domínguez dearly, and I want you to love her, and desire her, and nourish yourselves with the infinitely fragrant substances she brings us from afar.

Isn't that the destiny of bread and poetry?

—Pablo Neruda
Isla Negra, Chile
1973

Prólogo

Conocí a Delia Domínguez hace sólo treinta años, pero me parece que hemos estado juntas desde que ella era «una niña repolluda, que vivía en el campo con sus abuelos colonos, tenía la cara gorda y la peinaban —en un esfuerzo de bonitura— con crespos a lo Shirley Temple», como ella misma se describe con su gracia humilde.

Si yo hiciera su retrato, usaría colores espléndidos, verde de los bosques nativos y azul de los lagos y cielos del paralelo 40 sur, blanco de nieves eternas y tonos profundos de la tierra chilena. Así es su poesía, terrestre con raíces, aérea con alas de pájaro, translúcida como nuestras aguas.

Delia tiene sangre mestiza, una revoltura de mapuches, alemanes y chilenos; cuenta que su abuela Encarnación tenía los rasgos de Fresia y el carácter de Caupolicán.

Nació en la región de Los Lagos, custodiada por volcanes; por eso lleva magia por dentro. Habla como escribe, en verso y parábola. Se ríe desde lo profundo, llora y reza con cualquier pretexto, desconoce la mezquindad y va por el mundo regalando poemas, huevos frescos, hierbas de su huerto.

Su madre murió cuando tenía cinco años y le dejó un vacío tan pasmoso, que está convencida de que no sería poeta si ella hubiera vivido. Le faltaron manos de mujer. Para esa niña huérfana las palabras ocuparon el lugar de las caricias maternas. Aprendió a hablar y contestarse sola; vagaba por los campos con los perros, las gallinas, los gusanos. Sentía la ausencia de su madre como una injusticia tan inmensa, que nunca lograba tragar «la lágrima en la garganta». Se rebelaba, le daban épicas pataletas de dolor, que su abuelastra alemana procuraba aplacar atándola con tiras a los estribos de una yegua, donde solía pasar el día mirando al mundo desde la ira y la pena. De los indios aprendió a pensar en poesía. De ellos tiene hoy el apodo, la llaman Abuela Butahuillimapu, que significa vieja de las grandes tierras del sur.

Como todos los sabios, Delia cree en prodigios. Anda siempre «amilagrada» porque en su existencia muy pocos acontecimientos tienen explicación lógica; lo bueno y lo malo le pasa por puro capricho del destino. Eso la hace confiada y le da una especie de tranquila felicidad. Ya nada controla, no vale la pena angustiarse. Es transparente, como su poesía. Tiene olfato de perra patagónica y lo que no sabe, lo inventa. Para ella lo importante es la verdad y la ternura, es decir, el amor humano. Para el cariño no hay fronteras, ni divisiones de pelos o razas, sostiene. Le duele el desamor, le espanta la violencia «barata», esa dureza inútil que tanto ensucia al mundo. Está orgullosa de que a sus setenta y dos años de eterna juventud todavía tiene «el cerebro de atrás» en su lugar preciso.

Se siente abuela de los jóvenes poetas mapuche-huilliches, porque en ellos renació. Le creo, porque si vamos a hablar de reencarnación, esos poetas y Delia están unidos por la misma línea de luz. Como ellos, Delia es «licán», cuarzo que atrapa la pureza del sol... Delia es entendida en papas, en horarios de pájaros, en miel de abejas, ve debajo del agua, como los salmones. Vive en un caserón de ciento tres años, hecho de maderas firmes: laurel, coihüe, roble y pellín, un árbol noble como ella, que muere siempre de pie. Se cree afortunada, nunca le falla la suerte, dice, a pesar de sus encontronazos con la muerte y un pulmón reventado. Neruda la llamó «enérgica paloma de los montes» y le mandaba misivas en el chofer del bus que hacía el trayecto a Osorno por los caminos de aquellos tiempos.

Delia habla y respira en verso. A veces la sacudo, porque no aterriza en lo práctico, se tropieza, se confunde y, con un gesto que me desarma, confiesa que otra vez «la hicieron lesa». Con la edad, la poesía va invadiéndola, como la invade el soplo de Dios. Se acuesta y se levanta murmurando poemas propios y rezando por el gusto de dar las gracias. Cree que los versos se los dictan las ánimas y dice que sabe penar sin estar muerta, porque suele aparecerse ante personas que ama, aunque estén separadas por largas distancias. «Son cosas mágicas que pasan", me dice.

Le ofrecí escribir un prólogo para su libro *Clavo de olor*, pero me gasté el tiempo y las páginas contándoles de ella. No importa. Los poemas hablan por sí mismos. ¿Qué puedo decir que no sea mejor dicho por Delia?

—Isabel Allende

Prologue

I met Delia Domínguez only thirty years ago, but it seems to me that we have been together ever since she was "a stocky girl who lived in the countryside with her grandparents, who were colonists. She had a round face and they combed her hair—in an attempt to make her pretty—into Shirley Temple-style curls," as she describes herself with her humble grace.

If I were to paint her portrait, I would use splendid colors, the green of her native forests and the blue of lakes and skies at the 40th south parallel; the white of eternal snows and the deepest tones of the Chilean soil. That is what her poetry is: terrestrial with roots, aerial with the wings of birds, translucent like our waters. Delia has mestiza blood, a mixture of Mapuches, Germans, and Chileans; she says that her grandmother, Encarnacion, has characteristics of freesia and the character of Caupolicán.

She was born in the Lakes region, watched over by volcanoes, and therefore she carries magic within her. She talks the way she writes, in poetry and parable. She laughs from the depths, cries and prays at the slightest pretext, ignores pettiness and goes through life making gifts of poems, fresh eggs, and herbs from her garden.

Her mother died when she was five years old and left her with such incredible emptiness that she is convinced she would not be a poet had she lived. She was deprived of a mother's touch. For this orphaned child, words took the place of maternal caresses. She learned to talk and reply to herself; she wandered through fields with dogs, chickens, and worms. Her mother's absence felt like such a tremendous injustice that she never managed to swallow "the tears in her throat." She was rebellious; her sorrow produced epic tantrums that her German step-grandmother attempted to control by tying her with straps to the stirrups of a mare, where she would spend the day glaring at the world in anger and pain. From the Indians she learned to think in poetry. From them she received her nickname: they call her Grandmother Butahuillimapu, which means "old woman from distant southern lands."

Like all sages, Delia believes in miracles. She lives always "lost in wonder" because in her experience very few events have a logical explanation; good and bad befall her at the whim of fate. That makes her trusting and gives her a kind of calm happiness. Since she has no control over things, it is not worth suffering. She is transparent, like her poetry. She has the sense of smell of a Patagonian dog and what she doesn't know, she invents. What is important to her is truth and tenderness, that is, human love. There are no borders to affection, no divisions based on skin or race, she maintains. Indifference pains her; "cheap" violence, that needless callousness that defiles the world so much frightens her. She is proud that at her seventy-two years of eternal youth, "the back burners of her brain" are still firing.

She considers herself the grandmother of young Mapuche-Huilliche poets, because she was reborn through them. I believe her, because if we are going to talk about reincarnation, those poets and Delia are united by the same line of light. Like them, Delia is "licán," an indigenous plant, or quartz that traps the purity of the sun. Delia is understood through potatoes, in the timetables of birds, in honey from the bees; she sees beneath the water, like the salmon. She dwells in a spacious house, one hundred and three years old, made of hardwoods: laurel, *coihué*, oak and beech, a tree as noble as she is, that always dies standing tall. She considers herself fortunate; luck never fails her, she says, in spite of a punctured lung and her collisions with death. Neruda called her "an energetic mountain dove" and sent her missives in green ink, dripping with raindrops, via the bus driver who made the long journey to Osorno over the spiraling roads of those days.

Delia speaks and breathes in verse. Sometimes I shake her because she does not touch down on what is practical; she stumbles, becomes confused, and with a gesture I find disarming, confesses that again, "They cheated me." With age, poetry continues to infuse her, like the breath of God. She goes to bed and gets up whispering her own poems and praying for the pleasure of giving thanks. She believes her poems are dictated by souls and says she knows she is a specter without being dead because she is used to appearing to people she loves, even when they are separated by great distances. "There are magical things that happen," she tells me

I offered to write a prologue for her book, *Clavo de olor,* but I ran out of time and paper describing her. It doesn't matter. The poems speak for themselves. What can I possibly say that is not better said by Delia?

—Isabel Allende

Woman Without Background Music

El sol mira para atrás

En el cielo
el sol mira para atrás
porque tiene que llamar agua,
y tú conoces las señales
los sagrados olores de la tierra
y empiezas a lustrar tus botas
la escopeta del 16
que el abuelo colgó en el comedor
en ese otoño de su muerte.

Y en el moral huequeado por antiguos
          reventones de pólvora,
hay un juego de naipes gastados
como esa risa que fuimos perdiendo
cuando nos vendaron los sueños
para que creciéramos
más tranquilos, más ciegos,
y no preguntáramos
por qué el sol miraba para atrás
desde el umbral sonoro de la lluvia,
o por qué los que amábamos
no volvieron jamás
para justificar su eternidad
          a nuestro lado.
Y tú
y yo
tuvimos que ir guardando las sillas vacías
pasando llave
en el óxido de las chapas antiguas
pasándonos una costura en la boca
para quedarnos
con las palabras estrictamente necesarias
a nuestro sencillo amor.

The Sun Looks Back

In the sky
the sun looks back
because it must call the water,
and you know the signs
the sacred smells of the earth
and you begin to polish your boots
the 16-caliber shotgun
that grandfather hung up in the dining room
that autumn of his death.

And in the knapsack hollowed out by ancient
        explosions of powder
there is a deck of cards worn-out
like that laughter we kept on losing
when they blindfolded our dreams
so we would grow up to be
more calm, more unseeing
and we wouldn't ask
why the sun was looking back
from the sonorous threshold of the rain,
or why those we loved
never returned
to justify their eternity
        at our side.
And you
and I
had to begin putting away the empty chairs
turning the keys
in the rust of ancient locks
stitching our mouths closed
so we might be left
with only the words absolutely necessary
for our simple love.

El sol mira para atrás
porque tiene que llamar agua
y se ilumina la copa de los manzanos
y nos entra un frío por las rodillas
avisándonos la primera señal.

The sun looks back
because it must call the water
and the canopy of apple trees is illuminated
and a chill attacks our knees
the first sign warning us.

Esta es la casa

Esta es la casa
aquí la tienes con la puerta abierta
y los fogones encendidos.

Aquí vivo
conjurada por la noche de campo
y los mugidos de las vacas
que van a parir a la salida del invierno.
Entra en las piezas de sentimiento antiguo
con manzanas reinetas
y cueros claveteados en el piso.
Esta es la casa para ser como somos,
para contar las velas de cumpleaños
        y las otras también,
para colgar la ropa y la tristeza
que jamás entregaremos a la luz.

Este es el clima, niebla y borrasca,
sol partido entre los hielos
pero encima de todo:
un evangelio duro
una pasión sin vuelta
una carta de agua para la eternidad.

Esta es la zona: Km. 14, Santa Amelia,
virando hacia el oeste,
con todas las jugadas de la vida

This is the House

If someone wants to know what happens
to the rains in motion above
the earth, let him come live beneath my
roof, among the signs and omens.
                                            —Saint-John Perse

This is the house
here it is with the door open
and fires burning in the hearths.

I live here
conjured up by night in the countryside
and the lowing of cows
who'll give birth at the end of winter.
Come into rooms of vanished emotions
with fragrant yellow apples
and hides nailed to the floor.
This is the house where we can be what we are,
count birthday candles
            and others also,
hang up the clothing and sadness
we'll never expose to the light.

This is the climate, mist and storm,
sun split by glaciers,
but above all:
a cruel gospel
a passion without return
a letter in water for eternity.

This is the zone: Kilometer 14, Santa Amelia,
veering toward the west,
with all the dirty tricks of life

y todas las jugadas de la muerte.
Esta es la casa raspada por los vientos
donde culebreaban los inviernos
de pared a pared
de hijo a hijo
cuando nos aliviábamos con ladrillos caldeados
para aprender las sagradas escrituras
que la profesora de la Escuela Catorce
sacaba de un armario
o de los dibujos de un pañuelo.

Esta es la fibra fiel de la madera
donde calladamente me criaron
entre colonos y mujeres
que regresaron a su greda.

Aquí vivo con la puerta abierta
y este amor
que no sirve para canciones ni para libros,
con mi alianza sin ruido a Santa Amelia
donde puedes hallarme a toda hora
entre las herramientas y la tierra.

and all the dirty tricks of death.
This is the house scraped by the winds
where winters snaked their way
from wall to wall
from child to child
when we comforted ourselves with heated bricks
so we could learn the sacred scriptures
that the teacher from School 14
removed from a closet
or from the sketches on a handkerchief.

This is the faithful fiber of the wood
where they quietly raised me
among colonists and women
who returned to their clay.

Here I live with the door open
and this love
that's useless for songs or books,
with my silent alliance to Santa Amelia
where you can find me at any time
among my tools and the earth.

Mujer sin música de fondo

Estás ahí
cargada con el silencio de la vida
o con el silencio de la muerte,
y tu valentía se parece al viento
que nunca deja de soplar, y la cal
del muro te parte las mejillas,
y otras cosas
también te parten las mejillas:
> el peso de la sal
> lo que se traga y se atraviesa
> de costilla a costilla,
porque Padre Nuestro que estás en los cielos
a veces
se nos desploma el cielo en las narices
y una mujer puede quedar recostada en la noche
con el filo de un rayo entre los brazos.

Pero tú sabes qué hacer cuando se quiebra
> el pecho, y juras sin pestañear,
sin reclinar por eso la cabeza
y las huellas de todo lo que amabas
van haciéndose palomas
como tus ojeras enlutadas
donde las lágrimas
nunca se quedaron para siempre.

Estás ahí
con todo el amor en las rodillas
y tu fuerza aletea
sobre el humo de las fogatas en los campamentos
cuando las últimas linternas deben apagarse
y solo el corazón jinetea en la sombra.

Woman without Background Music

You're there
burdened with the silence of life
or with the silence of death,
and your valor resembles wind
that never ceases to blow, and the mortar
from the wall splits your cheeks,
and other things
also split your cheeks:
   the weight of salt
   what's swallowed and what passes
   from rib to rib,
because Our Father who art in heaven
sometimes
topples heaven into our faces
and a woman can wind up leaning into night
holding a lightning bolt in her arms.

But you know what to do when your heart's
   breaking, and so you swear without blinking,
without bowing your head
and the footprints of everything you loved
keep turning into doves
like the circles of mourning under your eyes,
where tears
never stayed forever.

You're there
with all your love in your knees
and your strength flutters its wings
above the smoke from bonfires in the camps,
where the last lanterns must be extinguished
and only the heart rides horseback in the shadows.

Y tú siempre velando
porque el cielo se te ha caído
como cincuenta veces sin música de fondo,
y a mí también se me ha caído
como granada de mano
hasta los reverendísimos alientos,
y eso era la mayoría de edad, decían,
cuando llegaba la hora de respondernos
de no arrancar ante el signo filudo del tiempo
            que picaba los sueños
donde recogíamos de a poco la esperanza.

Estás ahí,
partida en dos sobre la tierra
atravesada de hijos
de cicatrices costureadas
como los toldos de campaña
que esperaron el alba.

Estás ahí, sin música de fondo,
porque no necesitas la música de fondo,
apenas tu blusa azul
la libertad de movimientos
y la tierra que pisas.

And you're always vigilant
because the sky has fallen on you
at least fifty times without background music,
and it's also fallen on me
like a hand grenade
to the deepest sigh of despair,
and that was the coming-of-age, they said,
when the time came to respond,
never withdrawing faced with a sharp-edged sign of time
           that pierced the dreams
where we slowly gathered hope.

You're there,
split in two above the earth
run through by children
by scars stitched
like Indian tents
awaiting dawn in the countryside.

You're there, without background music,
because you don't need background music,
simply your blue blouse
freedom of movement
and the ground you walk on.

Adivino los sueños

Vendrán malas noticias
la leche se cortó antes de las 8,
yo soñé con aguas turbias, y las rodillas
me dolieron toda la santa noche.
Jaime mató el pitío anunciador
a la primera bala de su rifle
y no sé qué nieve de otro tiempo
se puso a blanquear el aire
y alguien dijo: 5 grados bajo cero
      se irán los afuerinos
      y quedaremos solos.

Hoy es sábado en el campo
y me acuerdo de otras cosas
avisadas por sueños:
      como la lombriz de perro
      la historia del pulmón
y esa muerte tuya en otro pueblo
cuando no pude llamarte
porque no había aprendido
todas las palabras.

I Divine Dreams

Bad news will arrive
the milk turned sour before 8,
I dreamed of murky waters, and my knees
were bothering me all the blessed night.
Jaime killed the bird of ill omen
with the first shot from his rifle
and some snow from another age
began to whiten the sky
and someone said: 5 degrees below zero
                    the outsiders will leave
                    and we'll be left alone.

Today is Saturday in the countryside
and I recall other things
foretold in dreams:
            like the dog's tapeworms
            the story of the lung
and that death of yours in another town
when I couldn't call you
because I hadn't learned
all the words.

Los frascos azules

No sé la historia de mis frascos azules
pero crecí con ellos
con las lenguas del sol en sus contornos
y el relumbre
en la humedad salada de mis ojos.
Allí filtró la luz sus abanicos
Cuando salimos de la infancia
y nos marcó la edad de golpe.

No sé la leyenda de los frascos,
una mano que amaba me los pasó en silencio:
eso fue todo. Alguien dijo una vez
que eran viajados, que tomaron el color del mar
cuando los colonos, hace ciento cincuenta años,
largaron sus velas en Hamburgo; que, a lo mejor,
estaban en la vidriería del pueblo
cuando llegaron los primeros espejos
y los floreros transparentes,
o que salieron de la memoria de un anciano
que los fue trasladando
con sus tabaqueras y sus rifles
por las repisas blanqueadas de las casas
que se quedaron a morir en la lluvia.

En los frascos azules guardo el aire
que te daré algún día
cuando todo sea verdad.

Blue Bottles

I don't know the history of my blue bottles
but I grew up with them
with tongues of sun in their contours
and their luster
in the salty dampness of my eyes.
There light filtered its fans
as we left childhood behind
and age suddenly left its mark on us.

I don't know the legend of the bottles,
a loving hand passed them to me in silence:
that was all. Someone once said
they were voyagers, that they took on the color of the sea
when colonists, one hundred fifty years ago,
unfurled their sails in Hamburg; that perhaps
they were in the windows of the town's glassware shop
when the first mirrors
and transparent vases arrived,
or that they arose from the memory of an old man
who was transporting them
with his tobacco pouches and his rifles
to the whitewashed mantelpieces of houses
that were left to die in the rain.

In blue bottles I preserve the air
I'll give you someday
when everything is true.

Nocturno con los pies helados

Tengo los pies helados
y nadie va a llegar con calcetines de lana
a hacerme compañía
porque ayer me cruzó la lechuza
de sur a norte en el camino
y sobrevoló hasta la medianoche
—como buen pájaro agorero—
a dos metros de la camioneta roja
donde traía los víveres del pueblo.

Tengo los pies helados
y corrieron por ahí
que desertaste por un canto de sirena.

Nocturne with Frozen Feet

My feet are frozen
and no one is going to come along with woolen socks
to keep me company
because yesterday an owl crossed my path
from south to north on the highway
and hovered overhead until midnight
—like a good bird of prophecy—
two meters from the red van
in which I was bringing provisions for the town.

My feet are frozen
and they ran through that place
you abandoned for a siren's song.

Conciencia

Cuando la pena se hizo conciencia
y apretamos los dientes
y nunca más tuvimos una almohada de sueños
            en el paraíso terrenal
porque a plena luz
las manos iban quedando vacías
y los cohetes
no eran—precisamente—señales
luminosos en el cielo,
y compartimos un vaso de vino
un pan
y le hiciste cariño a mi perro
y yo me estaba enfermando porque
tenía mucha niebla en el pecho;

cuando todo se nos fue volviendo esperanza;
me comprometí contigo
hasta la muerte.

Awareness

When grief became awareness
and we clenched our teeth
and never again had a pillow of dreams
        in this earthly paradise
because in the light of day
our hands were left empty
and the rockets
were not—exactly—luminous
signs in the sky,
and we shared a glass of wine
some bread
and you petted my dog
and I was growing ill because
my chest was filled with mist;

when everything was turning into hope for us,
I pledged myself to you
until death.

Tos de perro

Voy a decir aquí
que tengo tos de perro
para que alguien busque
        flores pectorales
y prepare un té caliente con malicia
y me emocione hasta los huesos,
como ese día lejano
casi perdido en los cajones
cuando bajábamos del cerro
y hablamos en secreto
emboscados en la complicidad de los aromos.
Pero la tos de perro es verdadera
como todo lo que sale en este verso
y mi pecho—si quieres saberlo—
es una caja de resonancias
donde silba el invierno,
y estará de Dios que me resigne
a esperar que alguna mano
haga hervir la tetera y me llene
de aromas esta casa, este pecho,
que necesita amor y compresas de franela
y cosas terriblemente reales,
como una voz
o el arco sumiso de tus brazos
para afirmar la noche.

Barking Cough

I'm going to say here
that I have a barking cough
so that someone will look for
            cough drops
and slyly prepare hot tea
and thrill me to my bones,
like that distant day
when we, almost lost in the canyons,
were descending the ridge
and speaking in secret
hidden in the forest in the complicity of myrrh trees.
But the barking cough is true
like everything that appears in this poem
and my chest—if you want to know—
is a soundbox
where winter whistles,
and it's God's will that I resign myself
to awaiting a hand
that will make the kettle boil and fill
with sweet smells this house, this chest of mine
that needs love and flannel compresses
and terribly real things,
like a voice
or the submissive arch of your arms
to hold fast the night.

Conversaciones al oído

I.
A las semillas, sin amor,
no les va a asomar el brote.

II.
La Ester dijo que era malo
barrer la sal que cae al piso
porque los escobazos llaman a los muertos.

III.
La Ester también le dijo a Francisco Coloane
que los brujos bailaban en el techo
cuando querían llevarse a su hermana
            enferma del pulmón.
Ella vio que les salía fuego por la boca
y que el novio maldito
le tiró la peste en una pera de agua
que le trajo del pueblo.

IV.
Si las quilas florecen este año,
estamos jodidos.

V.
Te haré nacer en mis poemas
y no te irás en hojas
como el maíz sembrado a destiempo.

VI.
La perdiz perdió la cola
porque asustó a la Santísima Virgen
y de ahí nacieron los remedos del diablo,
por ejemplo: Dios inventó el pescado

Conversations in One's Ear

I.
Without love, the bud will not become visible
to the seeds,

II.
Esther said it was bad luck
to sweep up salt that falls on the floor
because sweeping summons the dead.

III.
Esther also told Francisco Coloane
that witches were dancing on the roof
when they wanted to carry off his sister
        sick with lung disease.
She saw fire coming out of their mouths
and her damned boyfriend
infected her with the clap from an infection
he contracted in town.

IV.
If the bamboo blooms this year,
we're screwed.

V.
I'll give birth to you in my poems
and you won't disappear in leaves
like corn sown out of season.

VI.
The partridge lost its tail
because it frightened the Most Holy Virgin
and from that the devil's imitations were born,
for example: God invented fish,

y el Diablo la culebra,
Dios inventó los patos
y el Diablo sacó los cuervos.

VII.
El Orfeo—con todo respeto—
es el perro de cola mocha
que vigila mis sueños.

VIII.
Ya comenzaron a brotar los hongos
en el fondo del bosque
y cuando don Juan Navarro esta mañana
me trajo quintal al anca del caballo,
salí a besar la tierra
a desear que estuvieras conmigo
para guisarte los hongos con mis manos.

IX.
Un día de éstos me perderé en el bosque
para abrirle la jaula a mi silencio,
porque no voy a dar mis sueños por perdidos
ni mi corazón por muerto.

X.
Y cuando la lluvia cerrada
—aquí no hay tregua ni misericordia—
brillante las encinas y yo deba partir
con mis pulmones
detrás del sol o de tu olvido,
no pienses que me he destetado
para buscar la felicidad o el paraíso
porque mi cruz y mi alegría están aquí,

and the devil, snakes,
God invented ducks
and the devil created crows.

VII.
Orpheus—with all due respect—
is the dog with a cropped tail
who guards my dreams.

VIII.
Mushrooms have already begun to sprout
on the floor of the forest
and when Juan Navarro this morning
brought me a quintal of mushrooms on his horse's haunches,
I set out to kiss the earth
and wish that you were with me
so I could cook the mushrooms for you with my own hands.

IX.
One of these days, I'll get lost in the woods
and open the cage of my silence;
I won't accept that my dreams are lost
or my heart dead.

X.
And when the pouring rain
— there's neither truce nor compassion here—
makes the oak trees sparkle and I must depart
with my lungs
behind the sun or your oblivion,
don't think I've weaned myself from you
to search for happiness or paradise
because my cross and my joy are here,

mi oxígeno, mi gente del campo,
que con las manos cuarteadas
se encargó de mudarme los pañales
cuando murió mi madre.

XI.
Este año no se fueron las garzas
están aquí sobrevolando el tranque
a una cuarta de mi cabeza
interminables
como los sueños que tengo contigo.

XII.
A un lado del camino
permanecen los castillos de tablas mojadas
donde no se notan las lágrimas.

XIII.
Pero si las quilas florecen este año,
estamos jodidos.

XIV.
La Vicky del aserradero
dijo ayer que ella
no criaba sus hijos para bonitos
ni para andar fumando;
y de dos puñetes les compuso el cuerpo
para sacarles la angustia existencial.

my oxygen, my country folk,
who, with their broken hands,
took responsibility for changing my diapers
when my mother died.

XI.
This year the herons didn't leave
they're here hovering over the palisade
a short span above my head,
unending
like the dreams I have of you.

XII.
On one side of the road
stand castles of damp wooden boards
where tears aren't noticed.

XIII.
But if the bamboo blooms this year,
we're screwed.

XIV.
Vicky from the sawmill
said yesterday that she
wasn't raising her children to be pretty
or to go around smoking;
and with two punches to their bodies
she removed their existential anguish.

XV.

Y la Ester que venía en la micro rural
en el mismo asiento de doña Vicky
largó otro de sus versos proféticos:
    "perro que con luna se rasca la cola
    anuncia cadáver,"
y en ese rato pasó Chamelito Fernández
arando en el barro
con su bicicleta fantasma.

XVI.
Y este año
las garzas siguen pasando
lentas
solemnes
como los sueños que tengo contigo.

XV.
And Esther who arrived on the rural microbus
on the same seat as Vicky
delivered another of her prophetic lines:
     "A dog that scratches his tail by moonlight
     foretells a corpse,"
and at that moment Chamelito Fernández passed by
digging up the dirt
with his phantom bicycle.

XVI.
And this year
herons keep passing by,
slow
solemn
like the dreams I have of you.

Espacios interiores

Una pieza de paredes blancas
y la luz tamizada pasando
por las cortinas de crea cruda
a sentarse callada entre las sienes.
Una atmósfera de 5 de la tarde en el sur
pasos suaves en el piso encerado
y algo como lechoso y vago
—semisueño, tal vez—y los codos
firmes en la mesa de castaño
donde blanquea mi cuaderno
inmóvil
como la saliva en la boca de un muerto.

La pieza es un tiempo antiguo
una mano detenida en mi frente
una mariposa con frío.

Y este sur a las 5
siempre encajado en la niebla
como tirándome de la chaqueta.

Porque luego la puerta va a abirirse
y entrarán los perros a oler los cojines
cuando traigan la leña para estufa.
Después
Pasaré el cerrojo
y me veré con Malte en Ulsgaard
para la despedida de su abuelo.
Y yo no quiero saber qué día es éste
qué maldito día.

Interior Spaces

A room with white walls
and filtered light passing
through curtains of raw linen
to sit silently between my temples.
An atmosphere of 5 in the afternoon in the South
soft steps on the waxed floor
and something somewhat milky and hazy
—halfdream, perhaps—and elbows
planted firmly on the chestnut table
where my notebook remains blank
motionless
like saliva in the mouth of a dead man.

The room is a bygone time
a hand pausing on my forehead
a shivering butterfly.

And this South at 5 o'clock
always encased in mist
seems to be tugging on my jacket.

Because then the door will open
and the dogs will enter to sniff the cushions
when people bring firewood for the stove.
Then
I'll fasten the padlock
and I will see myself with Malte in Ulsgaard
bidding farewell to his grandfather.
And I don't want to know what day this is,
what damned day.

Pater de coelis deus

Siempre el agua, esta humedad
que empaña los vidrios
desde que tuvimos uso de razón,
los ojos enfermizos que nos hacían ver
              fantasmas
entre las sabanillas de la niebla
hasta afiebrarnos de soñar despiertos,
de oír graznidos
campanas de parroquias abandonadas
donde el viento había aflojado las ventanas,
responsos que llamaban a entierro:
PATER DE COELIS DEUS por los hermanos muertos
y otras voces veladas
que afinaron el tiempo.

Siempre la casa de postes labrados
afirmándose desde principios de siglo
en la lenta raíz de los abuelos,
y esas goteras en la claraboya
Strauss al anochecer cuando perdíamos
              la maldad ejercida en luz
y todo el firmamento era una música
              —para vivir o para morir—
valseando en la memoria, el piano
rendido a la nostalgia, el rezo,
y otros nudos de sal en la garganta,
Padre del cielo nuestro, los rituales
              de entonces
quebradizos como el recuerdo que nunca
podrá reconstruirse con la fidelidad
              que amábamos
porque todo está enterrado.

Pater de Coelis Deus

Always the water, this humidity
that's steamed up the windows
since we reached the age of reason
sickly eyes that made us see
          ghosts
between the quilts of mist
until we became feverish from daydreaming,
from hearing croaking
bells from abandoned parishes
where the wind loosened windows,
responses evocative of funerals.
PATER DE COELIS DEUS for our dead brothers
and other veiled voices
that ended the era.

Always the house with carved posts
affirming itself from the beginning of the century
in the slow root of our grandparents,
and those leaks in the transom
Strauss at twilight when we lost
          the evil exercised in daylight
and the entire firmament was a kind of music
          —for living or for dying—
waltzing in memory, the piano
surrendered to nostalgia, prayer,
and other lumps of salt in our throats.
Our Father in heaven, the rituals
          of that time
brittle like the memory that will
never be able to rebuild itself with the faithfulness
          we loved,
because everything has been buried.

Leche de mujer

El hijo de Dios
bajó a la tierra para hacerse hombre
y tuvo que buscar
el pecho de una mujer:
hiel y clavos por dentro y
          sólo la esperanza
sujeta a la sal seca de unos ojos
que jamás esquivaron la luz.

Ella
intemporal,
arrimó el recién nacido a sus pezones
y comenzó la vida de aquí abajo:

Ora pro nobis. . .

Mother's milk

The Son of God
descended to earth to become a man
and he had to search for
a woman's breast:
bile and nails within and
only hope
subject to the dry salt of some eyes
that never avoided the light.

She
eternal,
clutched the newborn to her nipples
and began his life here below:

Ora pro nobis. . .

Los felices duermen...

Los felices duermen con los ojos cerrados.
Los otros, con los ojos abiertos.

¿Cómo haces tú
cuando pones la cabeza en la almohada
y sabes, perfectamente,
que será tragedia griega juntar siquiera las pestañas
para inventar un sueño o un candor
más o menos decentes, mientras tu paisaje
es un borrón de manos y de rostros, una
acostada clandestina, y
te quedas en cero desvaneciéndote
como esas nubes donde se perdían los gansos salvajes
que veíamos pasar (con Nils Holgersson), una vez al año,
por los cielos del sur?

Happy People Sleep...

Happy people sleep with their eyes closed.
The others with open eyes.

What do you do
when you lay your head on your pillow
and know, perfectly well,
that it would be a Greek tragedy to close your eyes
simply to invent a more or less decent
dream or purity of mind while your landscape
is a blur of hands and faces, a
clandestine nap, and
you are left fading into nothingness
like those lost clouds of wild geese
we used to see (with Nils Holgersson) passing, once a year,
through the southern skies?

Silla de Viena

El reino no es el mismo,
sólo está Dios en todo lo que amabas.
Manos desconocidas tiran piedras al sueño:
no hay amparo posible.
Arriba pasan las aves de alas blancas
mientras el canto de los madereros
llega desde las barracas del oeste.

Algunos saludaron
con un toque de gorra esta mañana,
eran los nietos de los leñadores alemanes
que conociste en las casetas de relevo
cuando el bosque todavía era un gigante verde,
y en las tonelerías de Rahue Alto
se cargaban los vasos con pólvora del diablo.

El reino no es el mismo,
sólo está Dios en todo lo que amabas.
Los postigos del lado de la lluvia
se entornaron
el año que una mujer partió de negro,
y aún no sabes si la casa de tablas
está parada en este mundo, porque
disimulas tus fantasmas, cuando
lo que vale es el coraje
de hincarse a conversar de amor,
mientras se están muriendo tus raíces.

Abre el pestillo: un perro ciego
todavía dormita a los pies de tu silla de Viena.

Chair from Vienna

The kingdom is not the same,
God only exists in everything you once loved.
Unknown hands hurl stones at your dream:
no shelter is possible.
Above, white-winged birds pass by
while the song of the woodcutters
rises from cabins in the west.

Some who said hello
with a touch of their caps this morning,
were the grandchildren of the German woodcutters
you met in the poorhouses
when the forest was still a green giant
and in the cooperages of Rahue Alto
vessels were loaded with the devil's gunpowder.

The kingdom is not the same,
God only exists in everything you once loved.
The shutters on the house's rainswept side
were half-closed
the year a woman dressed in black departed,
and you don't know if the wooden house
still stands in this world because
you conceal your ghosts when
what matters is the courage
to kneel and speak about love
while your roots are dying.

Unbolt the door: a blind dog
still dozes at the foot of your chair from Vienna.

Pequeñas Profecías

Mañana, un Dios que no conozco
me ofrecerá la salvación, si es que no vendo mi alma
a la pasada de tu sombra.

Mañana, un vaho
subirá desde las plantaciones de maíz
y sabremos que está llegando otra estación encima,
porque la ropa se nos va a pegar por el lado de las costillas
y te irás para siempre
como esas visitas de la ciudad
que no conocen el arraigo ni el olor a hojas podridas
—ni mucho menos—
la desolación de las colinas
después de una maldita lluvia.

Mañana estaré muda,
vuelta hacia mi almohada solitaria
como una colegiala castigada en el ultimo rincón del mundo,
mientras las ortigas en el fondo del jardín
abrirán sus botones lechosos en la mitad de este silencio
cuando todo sea demasiado tarde.

Small Prophecies

Tomorrow, a God I don't know
will offer me salvation if I don't blindfold my soul
as your shadow passes by.

Tomorrow, a mist
will rise from the cornfields
and we'll know another season is upon us
because our clothing will stick to our ribs,
and you'll depart forever
like those visitors from the city
who don't know the sense of belonging or the scent of rotting
          leaves
—or even less—
the desolation of hillsides
after an infernal rain.

Tomorrow I'll be silent,
turned toward my solitary pillow
like a schoolgirl punished in the farthest corner of the world,
while the nettles at the back of the garden
will open their milky buttons in the midst of this silence
when it's all much too late.

Maitines

Un día
comenzó a moverse un limo en tu conciencia,
pero eras ciego aún
y no sabías que era imposible
vivir de soles apagados;
entonces
los maitines de los monjes trapenses
bajaron por los cajones de los cerros
a desvelarte por los siglos.
Y estás ahí, vulnerable
como un sietemesino con las mucosas lastimadas,
esperando que pase algún Mesías
a señalarte la puerta de salida
mientras te acurrucas en postura fetal
como perro con frío,
cuando nadie tendría por qué saber el color
de tus raspaduras interiores.

Matins

One day
slime began to move in your conscience
but you were still blind
and didn't know it was impossible
to live on extinguished suns;
then
the matins of the Trappist monks
descended through the canyons of the hills
to watch over you through the centuries.
And here you are, vulnerable,
like a premature child with a runny nose,
hoping some Messiah will pass by
to show you the exit door
while you curl up in a fetal position
like a dog who's cold,
when no one would need to know the color
of your internal scratchings.

Señal de partida

Todos los años, a la entrada del otoño,
el bramido del ciervo-gamo sube
hasta el techo de mi pequeña casa blanca
construida sobre postes labrados
en las vegas del sur.
El macho se cruza con las hembras
cuando el barómetro anuncia las primeras heladas
en el empavonado de los vidrios.
Entonces
sé que debo partir hacia las tierras altas
de un norte más caliente.

Sign of Departure

Every year, at the coming of autumn,
the roar of the stag rises
to the rooftop of my little white house
built on posts carved
in the forests of the south.
The male mates with the females
when the barometer announces the first frosts
in the blurred frames of windowpanes.
Then
I know I must leave for the highlands
of a warmer north.

Dios es nuestro amigo

Como Dios es nuestro amigo
y las cartas del cielo han sido buenas este año
y ningún cartucho ha reventado a medianoche
los sueños de las mujeres embarazadas;

Yo confío
(igual que un niño en la mirada de su perro)
en tu capacidad de reconocer las señales de este amor,
con la misma precision
que los movimientos de la Novena Sinfonía
de Ludwig van Beethoven.

God is Our Friend

Since God is our friend
and the signs from heaven have been good this year
and not a single cartridge has burst
the dreams of pregnant women at midnight;

I trust
(like a child in the gaze of his dog)
in your ability to recognize the signs of this love
with the same precision
as the movements of the Ninth Symphony
by Ludwig van Beethoven.

Agua de hierbas

Los ancianos que murieron
tomaban hierba de Artemisa
para aclarar sus aguas interiores.

¿Y si el mundo tomara hierba de Artemisa?
(Crece silvestre al sur del paralelo 40).
A lo mejor
estaríamos todos frente a frente
limpios
como recíen nacidos.

Herbal Tea

The old people who died
drank Artemisa tea
to purify their vital fluids.

And what if the world drank Artemisa tea?
(It grows wild south of the 40th parallel).
Perhaps
we'd all be facing each other
pure
as newborn babes.

Sueño con peces

Sueño con peces que mueren en mis manos,
con campos de lavanda
donde el sol descarga su nuez envenenada,
y tú
        bella y lejana
juegas
como si no estuvieras boca abajo
        en el fondo del lago
desde esa maldita hora de perros.

I Dream of Fish

I dream of fish that die in my hands,
of fields of lavender
where the sun unleashes its poisoned nut,
and you
        beautiful and distant
play
as if you were not face down at
        the bottom of the lake
ever since that damned bitch of a time.

Auto-retrato

Soy como los animales:
presiento la desgracia en el aire
y no duermo sobre arenas movedizas.

Arriba siempre el viento
—desde el tiempo de los pañales mojados—
raspando la solidez de los cartilagos
mientras alguien
con mano sosegada escribe en mi cuaderno
cortas palabras de tristeza.

Soy como los animales:
sé pisar en la oscuridad, y
desde el fin del mundo,
podría volver con los ojos vendados
a mi vieja casa en las Colinas.

Los años cortan
agazapados por dentro,
pero se desvanece el miedo a estas alturas
y una opalina
filtra su luz en el salón del piano
donde danzan mis muertos con su sombra.

Soy como los animales de narices mojadas:
olfateo en el cielo
la carga de la tormenta eléctrica
y desconfío de pasos que no conozco.

Soy como los animales:
siento que empiezo la vuelta a mi tierra de origen...

¡Cristo sabrá por qué!

Self-Portrait

I'm like the animals:
I sense misfortune in the air
and I don't sleep on shifting sands.

Above, the wind, always
—since the time of damp diapers—
scratching the solidity of the cartilage
while someone
with a soothing hand writes in my notebook
short words of sadness.

I'm like the animals:
I know how to step lightly in the darkness, and
from the ends of the earth,
I could return with my eyes blindfolded
to my former home in the hills.

The years cut,
huddled inside,
but fear vanishes at this stage,
and an opalescence
filters its light in the music room
where my dead ones dance with their shadows.

I'm like the animals with moist nostrils:
I sniff in the sky
the charge of the electrical storm
and distrust footsteps I don't know.

I'm like the animals:
I sense I'm beginning the return to my land of origin...

Only Christ knows why!

En las encinas canta el tucuquere

Todo está inmóvil,
en las encinas canta el tucuquere
y el cuarto-creciente
es otro acto de magia donde no toco fondo.

Todo está inmóvil,
una niña con delantal de brin
se para a conversar con la abuela muerta
en los círculos rojos de la luna:
un corredor vacío
y los últimos ecos de un disco de post-guerra
en la victrola de los años cuarenta
me cortan las palabras.

Todo está inmóvil en la noche del sur,
como esperando una señal de partida
que, a lo mejor, no escucharemos;
solo el tucuquere encrespa sus penachos
en la oscuridad de un árbol hueco
y canta.

El tucuquere no conoce el sol,
tal vez un rayo enlutó sus ojos para siempre.
El tucuquere-buho no anuncia desgracias
solamente llama
desde los pozos de la noche.

In the Oak Trees the Owl Sings

All is still,
in the oak trees the horned owl sings,
and the waxing moon
is another act of magic where I don't touch bottom.

All is still,
a girl with an apron made of horsehair
stops to chat with her dead grandmother
in the red circles of the moon:
an empty corridor
and the last echoes of a record from the post-war period
on a victrola from the forties
cut off my words.

All is still in the southern night,
as if awaiting a signal of departure
that perhaps we won't hear;
only the horned owl ruffles its feathers
in the darkness of a hollow tree
and sings.

The owl doesn't know the sun,
perhaps a bolt of mourning darkened its eyes forever.
The horned owl doesn't announce misfortunes,
it only calls
from the wells of the night.

Cuadro de comedor

El comedor vacío de personas,
cuadro real: no invento nombres para la salvación eterna,
Soy la hojarasca del último verano
aquí en la pieza de paredes blancas
donde un cuero de zorro
y una frutera de vidrio me acompañan.

Oscurece en el Sur,
cuadro real: una mujer amaneció tirada en una fosa
y comenzaron todas las desgracias.

Los ojos de las fotografías cada vez más adentro.
Las palabras no dicen lo que pronuncian las palabras:
hay que aprender las claves del silencio.

El comedor vacío de personas,
cuadro real: me sube el frío por la espalda como una lagartija.
(Se fue la mano que extendía las mantas).
Un plato, un vaso, la sal cristalizada
debajo de mi lengua.

"Ropa gruesa para la soledad" decían las ancianas
cuando estiraban sus refajos en tiempo del deshielo
y llovía 40 días y 40 noches
y el río era un tambor de guerra
bombardeando los tímpanos.

El comedor vacío de personas,
cuadro real: estoy aquí para no falsear
paraísos terrenales, para tomar mi sopa,
sin máscaras ni cuero de gallina.

Dining Room Portrait

Dining room devoid of people,
a real portrait; I don't invent names for eternal salvation.
I'm the leaf storm from last summer
here in the room with white walls
where a fox pelt
and a glass fruit bowl keep me company.

It's getting dark in the south,
a real portrait: a woman awakened was thrown into a pit
and every misfortune began.

The eyes in the photographs more and more inward.
Words don't mean what they say:
one must recognize clues of silence.

Dining room devoid of people,
a real portrait: cold creeps up my back like a lizard.
(The hand that spread the tablecloth has gone.)
A plate, a glass, salt crystallized
beneath my tongue.

"Heavy clothing for loneliness" the old women would say
when they stretched wearing their slips beyond the thaw,
and it rained 40 days and 40 nights
and the river was a drum of war
bombarding the eardrums.

Dining room devoid of people,
a real portrait; I'm here to not misrepresent
earthly paradises, to eat my soup,
without masks or goosebumps.

Estoy con los retratos de los viejos colonos,
con Gustav Mahler (*Das Lied von der Erde*),
y un chal tirado sobre mis botas húmedas;
oigo las liebres que suben desde el plantío
hasta este cuadro de comedor
donde no estoy pintada:

donde vivo.

I'm with the portraits of former colonists
with Gustav Mahler (*Das Lied von der Erde*),
and a shawl tossed over my damp boots;
I hear rabbits approaching from the planted fields
toward this dining room portrait
where I'm not painted:

where I live.

Vals de "Libre Pensamiento"

Antiguamente, los jóvenes y las muchachas
iban a los salones iluminados
de las grandes casas de tres pisos
con sus mejores ropas de domingo. Una orquesta
cambiaba los silencios por compases de Strauss o de Franz Lehár,

pero, lo más hermoso, contaba mi padre,
era el "Vals de libre pensamiento"
cuando las mujeres elegían al hombre
para deslizarse sobre las "Ondas del Danubio."

Mucho más tarde
en la kermesse de la provincia,
yo recuerdo a la señorita del piano,
imperturbable, con sus senos parados de abundancia
tocando hasta el amanecer, y al polaco del violín
soñando a ojos cerrados con romances lejanos
mientras el sudor manchaba su frac
traído desde Europa en un baúl de los antepasados.

Hoy, nadie va a los salones de las grandes casas;
ellas murieron bajo la lluvia con sus ventanas ciegas
como los amores de entonces.

Hoy, nadie pide un "Vals de libre pensamiento",
no hay tiempo, ni señorita del piano, ni silencio
para cambiarlos por compases de música bailable.

Andamos solos,
alguien nos reventó los tímpanos de golpe
con un barril de pólvora cuando los que amábamos
nos abandonaron para siempre.

"Progressive Thinking" Waltz

In days gone by, young men and women
would go to salons of the illuminati
in great three-story homes
in their best Sunday clothing. An orchestra
exchanged the silences for rhythms by Strauss or Franz Lehár,

but, the most beautiful thing, my father would tell me,
was the "Progressive Thinking" waltz
where the woman chose the man
to glide on "Waves of the Danube".

Much later
at a kermess in the province,
I remember the young woman playing piano,
undisturbed, her abundant breasts erect,
playing until dawn, and the Polish violin player
dreaming with closed eyes of faraway romances
while sweat stained his tuxedo,
brought from Europe in his ancestors' trunk.

Today, no one goes to salons in the great houses;
they perished beneath the rain, their windows blind
as the loves of former times.

Today, no one requests a "Progressive Thinking" waltz,
there's no time, nor a young woman pianist, nor silence
to exchange for the rhythms of dance music.

We travel alone.
Someone burst our eardrums
with a barrel of gunpowder when those we loved
abandoned us forever.

Pido que vuelva mi ángel

En nombre de todo lo perdido
de los cometas que nunca más volvieron
a señalar caminos con sus colas de fuego
porque la muerte se paseó en puntillas
desde el pecho de una mujer que pudo amarnos:
pido que vuelva mi ángel.

Por la maleza que cubrió los patios
donde se hundió la luz como canción de cuna
y nuestra soledad fue canto de lechuzas
en el retumbadero de la noria:
pido que vuelva mi ángel.

Por las estufas apagadas en las cocinas del sur
donde los paños bordados en punto de cruz
conservan la lengua de Goethe
en estrictas sentencias que todos olvidaron:
pido que vuelva mi ángel.

Por las manos de hombre
que cargaban antiguas escopetas de caza
y tendían cueros de venado sobre las camas frías
en los dormitorios mojados del invierno:
pido que vuelva mi ángel.

Por los que compartieron nuestra cena,
y probaron el pan y la sopa de la felicidad
cuando aún ninguna muerte
tomaba asiento a nuestro lado
y creíamos ser los héroes de una juventud eterna:
pido que vuelva mi ángel.

I Beg my Angel to Return

In the name of all that's lost,
of comets that never returned
to show us the way with their fiery tails
because death strolled on tiptoe
from the breast of a woman who could have loved us:
I beg my angel to return.

For the sake of the weeds that covered the courtyards
where light was buried like a lullaby
and our loneliness was the song of owls
in the roar of the waterwheel:
I beg my angel to return.

For the sake of stoves extinguished in southern kitchens
where tapestries embroidered in crosstitch
preserved the language of Goethe
in strict maxims that all forgot:
I beg my angel to return.

For the sake of a man's hands that
carried antique hunting rifles
and placed deerskin hides on the cold beds
in bedrooms dampened by winter:
I beg my angel to return.

For the sake of those who shared our supper,
and tasted the bread and soup of happiness
when no death had yet
taken a seat by our side
and we believed ourselves the heroes of an eternal youth:
I beg my angel to return.

Por el amor, al fin, por el olvido
y lo que fue verdad en el entierro de los sueños,
por ti y por mí, temblando de esta maldita soledad,
visibles desde lejos en el paraíso terrenal:
pido que vuelva mi ángel.

For the sake of love, finally, for oblivion
and for what was true in the burial of our dreams,
for you and for me, trembling in this cursed loneliness,
visible from afar in the earthly paradise:
I beg my angel to return.

Caldo de Cultivo

Yo, caminando con los ojos cerrados pero no soy sonámbula.
Yo, atorada de tanta mudez ensartada al pescuezo
en la hiperrealidad de la natura: caldo de cultivo.

Y, más todavía, con un trapo amarrando el quejido
que a lo major es parto o muerte que me baila
—no sé bien cómo entra la vida o
cómo entra la muerte al baile—
y en beneficio de la duda: caldo de cultivo.

Y, después, yo con los ojos abiertos
cuando alguien mentó mi nombre en mitad del sueño
y, eso es malo para la cordura, puede morir
de ataque,
dijeron y yo colgando entre una cosa y otra
es decir entre nacida y no nacida
es decir en el limbo: caldo de cultivo.

Y, yo agarrada a mi fe de bautismo
perteneciente a: todos los patos silvestres
a la olla de los grandes lagos
a los repollos corazón de buey
a los cielos eléctricos mi columna vertebral,
perteneciente al vals inacabable de Strauss,
a los bosques de Viena a la chilena
a mis solos de piano machacados llorando a
la chilena: caldo de cultivo.

Y, yo acorralada en mi geografía de fin de mundo,
sin disimular la ojera metafísica de esta vigilia,
amanecida como viuda de Dios en pos del
amor eterno: caldo de cultivo.

Breeding Ground

I walk with my eyes closed but I'm not a sleepwalker.
I'm choked by so much silence wound around my neck
in the hyperreality of nature: breeding ground.

And, what's more, with a gag holding back the moaning
which perhaps is labor or death that waltzes me around
—I don't really know how life or
death enters the dance—
and for the benefit of the doubt: breeding ground.

And afterwards, with my eyes open,
someone mentioned my name in the midst of sleep
and that is bad for one's sanity, you might die of an attack,
they said, and I was suspended between one thing and another
I mean between being born and not being born
I mean in limbo: breeding ground.

And, clutching my baptismal faith
belonging to: all the wild ducks
the seething cauldron of the great lakes
the oxheart cabbages
the electrical skies, my spine,
belonging to Strauss's never-ending waltz,
the Viennese woods, Chilean style
my pounded piano solos crying out
Chilean style: breeding ground.

And I corralled in my geography of the end of the earth
without disguising the metaphysical circle under this vigil's eye,
dawning like the widow of God in pursuit of
eternal love: breeding ground.

Y, yo con 500 años sacando pecho
desde el gran diluvio hasta este otro diluvio
hilvanada de cantos y espantos como enagua de vieja:
caldo de cultivo.

Y, por último vulnerable como polla de un día
semiperdida en el jardín de Rilke
en los jardines—cementerio
de los colonos del sur, precisando al Jesús que
desciende
pre-ci-san-do porque no hay quien aguante
no hay quien (aguante) con un pie arriba y el
otro abajo para siempre: caldo de cultivo.

And I 500 years old striving to survive
from the great flood until this other flood
stitched together with chants and phantoms like an old woman's
petticoat: breeding ground.

And finally vulnerable as a new-born chick
half lost in Rilke's garden
in the cemetery gardens
of the southern colonists, needing Jesus who
descends
need-ing because there is no one who can bear it
there is no one (who can bear it) with one foot above and the
other below forever: breeding ground.

Papel de antecedentes

Yo, católica mestiza
minimalista y campesina.

Yo, perrera y jineta del viento de ombligo
amarrado a la telúrica madrecita tierna
de nunca acabar.

Yo, de sesenta para arriba y para abajo
me sé de corrido los Diez Mandamientos,
El Ojo (o-j-o) y la *Pastoral* de L. Van Beethoven.

Role of Ancestors

I Catholic mestiza
minimalist and country dweller.

I dog-fancier and horsewoman   my center of gravity bound to
the telluric never ending
tender little mother.

I sixty through and through
know by heart the Ten Commandments,
the Eye (e-y-e) and L. van Beethoven's *Pastoral.*

Veo la suerte por las yeguas

Se revuelcan las yeguas en el pasto ovillo como jugando
como muriendo las yeguas.

No se paran las yeguas, yo digo es la malura,
yo digo alguien muere hoy
algo grande va a pasar aquí si no se paran pronto
estas yeguas mulatas
que me trajinan por el sistema arterial
por el hueso sacro
por el sistema cerebro-inmemorial
con toda la historia de la casa como las Polonesas
el Danubio y la Marcha Triunfal.

Las señales no mienten,
si no se paran las yeguas se nubla toda la suerte.
Naipe revuelto a estas alturas
nadie puede ordenar a los hijos del paraíso.

Todo es un galope de yeguas volteadas
sobre el óxido empastado de América del Sur.

I See Fate through the Mares

The mares tumble about in the new grass as if playing
as if dying, the mares.

The mares don't stop, I say it's spasms,
I say someone's dying today
something big is going to happen here if they don't stop soon
these mulatto mares
that hustle and bustle through my circulatory system
through my sacrum
through my immemorial cerebral system
with the entire history of the house like the Polonaises
the Danube and the Triumphal March.

The signs don't lie,
if the mares don't stop fate will all become clouded.
Overturned card at this stage
no one can command the children of paradise.

Everything is a gallop of mares tumbling
over the weed-covered rust of South America.

Réquiem

Si volvemos a vernos quiero
ir otra vez a la escuela.
—B. Brecht

Un niño rosado viene saliendo de su hueco en el cielo.
Al mismo tiempo un viejo tirita porque
no sabe si tendrá hueco en el cielo mientras
en los reclinatorios de la capilla de campo, los pájaros,
a picotazo limpio han venido a cubrir a las pájaras
en un acto sagrado, como si supieran que ellos
tienen destapados todos los huecos del cielo.

Y, entre el niño y el viejo
me encontré por última vez con Hilda May,
alumbrada de rojo-negro cual Paloma Picasso,
hincada en los reclinatorios
de la capilla de campo, segura de su tiempo,
de que estaba empezando un vuelo recto
hacia su propio hueco en el cielo.

Pero, yo no sé si el tiempo del hombre
es igual al tiempo de los pájaros.

Requiem

If we see each other again, I want
to go to school once more.
—B. Brecht

A rosy child comes along, emerging from his niche in heaven.
At the same time an old man shivers because
he doesn't know if he'll have a niche in heaven   while
in the prie-dieux of the country chapel, the male birds,
savagely pecking have come to cover the female birds in
a sacred act, as if they knew that they
have uncovered all the niches of heaven.

And between the child and the old man
I found myself for the last time with Hilda May, illuminated
with
red-black like Paloma Picasso, kneeling in the prie-dieux
of the country chapel, certain of her time,
certain she was beginning a direct flight toward her
own niche in heaven.

But I don't know if man's time
is the same as the time of the birds.

Santísima Trinidad

En el nombre del Padre
del Hijo
del Espíritu Santo, y
de esta frazada para taparnos del frío.

En la lengua,
cortadas todas las palabras
como si el tiempo que estanca la luz
en los ojos de una moribunda
espiara los movimiento de amor, los roces
de pies y manos,
la razón agresiva de mi mudez
francamente en peligro.

Y a esta hora
leve como pisada de zorro en la escarcha,
cuando en nombre de la Santísima Trinidad
debes irte sin volver la cabeza;
te digo que la revelación puede andar de
Caperucita en el bosque, de monja, o
de poeta maldito,
aunque todavía no vislumbres la señal
encajonada en cierta palabra
que por ahora no puedo escribirte.

Most Holy Trinity

In the name of the Father
and the Son
and the Holy Spirit, and
this blanket that covers us from the cold.

On my tongue,
all words cut off
as if time that stanches the light
in the eyes of a dying woman
might spy the movements of love, the friction
of feet and hands,
the aggressive reason of my silence
frankly in danger.

And at this hour
light as the step of a fox on the hoar-frost,
when in the name of the Most Holy Trinity
you should leave without turning your head;
I tell you that revelation may walk like
Little Red Riding Hood in the forest, like a nun, or
like a cursed poet,
even though you may not yet glimpse the signal
trapped in a certain word
that for now I cannot write down for you.

Puros pastos

El rayo verde sale de los pastizales
la conexión eléctrica de mi geografía
pintada al agua semi hundida
en estos pozos del fin del mundo.

El paisaje de frente es la llanura de puros pastos.
El paisaje de espaldas es la llanura de puros pastos.

No queda otra
se moja el pañal entre las piernas.
Tengo miedo, estoy cosechada hace rato.
Mi hazaña es
será chupar algo de la savia de los pastos

encajarme en el cielo de las abonaduras
nacer para atrás
a ver si me meto otra vez
en el útero de la mía—nuestra madre
de los puros pastos.

Purely Pastures

A green lightning bolt erupts from the pasturelands
the electrical connection of my geography
reflected in the water half drowned
in these wells at the ends of the earth.

The landscape in front is a plain purely of pastures.
The landscape in back is a plain purely of pastures.

No other remains
the cloth between my legs grows damp.
I'm afraid, I've been harvested for a while.
My great deed is
will be to suck some sap from the pastures

to squeeze myself into the cycle of abundance
to be born in reverse
to see if I enter again
the uterus of what is mine—our mother
purely of pastures.

Abre los ojos / Cierra los ojos
(acto de magia)

O sea, entrecierra las vistas
parada-sentada 100 años
como abuela huilliche atizando la llama.

Así el color de la memoria
será un retrato desvaído de la in-memoria,
un borrón afiebrado un cuento
de revoltura entre vivientes y finados tu cuento.

Por eso, abre los ojos / cierra los ojos vuélvete mágica
que entre lo que veas y lo que no veas
puede estar el sentido de esta iluminación, o sea,
tú ahí, parada-sentada con una costura en la boca,
sabia y hermosa como las abuelas huilliches.

Open Your Eyes / Close Your Eyes
(act of magic)

That is, gaze at the scene through half-closed eyes
standing-sitting 100 years
like a Huilliche grandmother stirring the flames.

Thus the color of memory
will be a faded portrait of non-memory
a feverish smudge a story
of intermingling the living and the dead
your story.

Therefore, open your eyes/close your eyes become magical
so that between what you may see and what you may not
may be the meaning of this illumination, or rather,
you here, standing-sitting, biting off threads with your teeth,
wise and beautiful like the Huilliche grandmothers.

Unos arriba y otros abajo

No estaba ni vivo ni muerto,
y no sabía nada, mirando en silencio
dentro del corazón de la luz.
—T.S. Eliot, *La Tierra Baldía*.

El sueño es una mancha de barro
sobre el vidrio empavonado del bosque,
una hora hueca donde no toco fondo.

Todo flota
nadie puede pararse sobre sus propios pies,
nadie cierra los ojos porque están llenos de agua
y hasta los más juiciosos
amanecen con la pupila rebalsada en este pueblo
donde la lluvia se quedó a cuajar sus yemas
para siempre

donde los vivos y los muertos
son una mancha de barro sin mucha diferencia

nada más que
unos están arriba y otros abajo
de la paciencia de Dios.

Some Above and Others Below

...I was neither
Living nor dead, and I knew nothing,
Looking into the heart of light, the silence.
—T.S. Eliot, *The Waste Land*

The dream is a muddy stain
on the steel blue glass of the forest,
an empty hour where I can't touch bottom.

Everything floats
no one can stand on his own feet,
no one closes his eyes because they're filled with water
and even the most judicious
awaken with their pupils dammed up in this town
where the rain remained to harden their hearts
forever

where the living and the dead
are a muddy stain without much difference

except that
some are above and others below
God's patience.

Sabidurías de gallinero III
(En lo tocante al amor y a su galaxia)

Las estrellas cuando mueren dejan un hoyo negro.
Los que amamos cuando mueren dejan un hoyo negro.
Pero si tú mueres y yo muero
no quedará un hoyo negro sino una astrología en
la carta cósmica una escritura tan elemental
que podrá ser leída hasta por los niños que no
saben leer.

Esta vendría siendo mi sabiduría, mi física cuántica,
en lo tocante a la galaxia, a la ecuación poética resuelta
como sigue: "escribir por ejemplo, la noche está estrellada
y tiritan azules los astros a lo lejos."

Henhouse Wisdom III
(As regards love and its galaxy)

Stars when they die leave a black hole.
Those we love when they die   leave a black hole.
But if you die and I die
a black hole won't remain but rather an astrological sign in
the cosmic chart a writing so elementary
it can be read even by children who don't
know how to read.

This would become my wisdom, my quantum physics,
with regards to the galaxy, to the poetic equation resolved
as follows: "Writing, for example, the night is starry
and the stars blink blue in the distance."

Introducción

¿Esto es un prólogo?

No. Es una imitación de prólogo. A estas alturas del concierto, pensé que era prudente asumir con las arrugas de mi ropa el trajín del presente y del pasado.

¿Y por dónde ha trajinado ultimamente?

Por los barrancos sin fondo de la Sur-América, donde el cristiano es relincho mestizo y animita con techo de dos aguas en todos los caminos.

Hablando de animitas ¿sospecha de algún paraíso por aquí cerca, para gloria de las almas pías?

Poco tengo de píadosa pero, sospecho. Pienso que llegaré al paraíso porque sé dónde empieza el arcoiris de tanto escampar entre las piernas de la lluvia. Eso se aprende desde el ombligo, sin ser muy avisada de cabeza.

¿Y cuál sería la forma de avisarle directamente a la cabeza?

Comprometiéndose hasta la molleja con el humano que asiste a la misma película que uno, sin prejuiciar.

Con fe de pájara silvestre.

¿Y quiénes vendrían siendo aquellas pajaritas?

Entre muchas que vuelan en bandadas, mismamente yo.

Entonces, ¿podría revelar el método para no caer baleada de alas en la revoltura de un siglo a otro, sobre todo, ante la nueva metafísica del verbo, esa que arruga las entretelas del cerebro?

Yo no conozco el método. Se acabaron las recetas porque, al final, la persona bate los huevos a su aire sin ceñirse a reglas ñoñas.

Por ejemplo, el caso de Benjamín Subercaseaux quien, fuera de las pautas legales, exigía su propia sartén de fierro, oliva virgen y, pimienta de cayena.

¿Sería todo?

Sería."

—D.D.

Introduction

Is this a prologue?

No. it's an imitation of a prologue. At this late stage of the con-
cert, I thought it was wise to take on, along with the wrinkles of
my clothing, the hustle and bustle of present and past.

And where have you hustled and bustled about lately?

In the endless gorges of South America, where Christians are stub-
bornly undecided mestizo souls resting between two worlds, wher-
ever they go.

Speaking of little souls, do you suspect some paradise nearby, for
the glory of pious souls?

I'm hardly pious, but I suspect so. I think I'll reach paradise because
I know where the rainbow begins between the legs of the rain.
That's known in your gut, without being informed very much by
your head.

And how would you inform your head directly?

Committing yourself up to the gizzards to the human being who
goes to the same movie you do, without prejudging.

With the faith of a wild bird.

And who might those little birds be?

Among the many who fly in flocks, even I myself.

Then, could you reveal a way of not winding up shot in the wings
in the flux from one century to another, facing the new meta-
physics of the word, the one that wrinkles the core of your brain?

I don't know the way. Recipes are useless, because, in the end, each
person beats eggs his own way without following foolish rules.

For example, the case of Benjamin Subercaseaux, who, outside offi-
cial guidelines, demanded his own iron frying pan, virgin olive oil,
and cayenne pepper.

Could that be all?

It could be.

—D.D.

Regla de tres

Se puede nacer de a dos
pero se muere de a uno.

Rule of Three

You can be born by twos
but you die by ones.

Poema de los polos

Me gustan las latitudes extremas, trátense de
árticas o antárticas.

Ellas entregan al ojo, el mapa astral
de los puntos cardinals,
la música de las esferas, para que
no se desorienten las animas en pena.

Si nó, pregúntele a Sibelius,
a Knut Hamsun,
a Neruda y Coloane,
o mejor
a la Filarmónica del Cabo de Hornos
dirigida por el último yagán.

Después hablamos.

Poem of the Poles

I like the extreme latitudes, whether they are
Arctic or Antarctic.

They surrender to the eye the astral map
of the cardinal directions,
the music of the spheres, so
the souls in purgatory don't become disoriented.

If you don't agree, ask Sibelius,
Knut Hamsun,
Neruda and Coloane,
or even better
the Cape Horn Philharmonic
directed by the last Yagán.

Then we'll talk.

Todas las mujeres son mi madre

Todas pero, yo también,
soy la madre de todas.
No tengo tragedias sicológicas ni teológicas, y
Jamás he perdido la conciencia
de la sangre que
sube
y de la sangre que baja madre.

Eso sí, me confieso
Vulnerable como sietemesina
pero, a la vez, fuerte como olla de tres patas

donde
hierven
todos
los
caldos
de
Chile.

All Women are My Mother

All of them, but, I too,
am the mother of them all.
I don't have psychological or theological tragedies, and
I've never lost awareness
of the blood that
rises
and the blood that falls mother.

However, I do admit to being
vulnerable as a premature child
but, at the same time, strong as a three-legged stewpot

where
all
the
broths
of
Chile
boil.

Realismo mágico

A María Luisa Bombal

Borges dijo: "a lo major somos un sueño
y esa sería nuestra realidad."

Entonces no hay que partirse la cabeza
ni patalear de miedo. Cada noche
un arcángel sale del huevo de Dios,
nos pone alas y así descubrimos la
irrealidad que viene a ser
       la misma realidad.

Magical Realism

To María Luisa Bombal

Borges said, "Perhaps we are a dream
and that must be our reality."

Then there's no need to drive yourself crazy
or kick up a fuss out of fear. Every night
an archangel emerges from God's egg,
gives us wings and thus we discover the
unreality that becomes
reality itself.

Los niños de la lluvia

Todo el día escucho el ruido de las aguas
sollozando.
—James Joyce

Los niños de la lluvia suben y bajan por
el filón que inventa la luna en las colinas.

Los niños de la lluvia son nietos
de la abuela mestiza que se quedó a morir
en las casas de alerce que orillean el lago.
Los niños saben pisar en los pantanos como
caballos ciegos. Pero al menor descuido
se convierten en flechas
        o en enanos fantasmas.

Los niños de la lluvia
        son más surrealistas que Breton,
más viejos y más niños que Huidobro:
        me pregunto otra vez, ¿irían a ser mudos
        que Dios les dio esos ojos...?
Los niños de la lluvia no son malos ni buenos
perjuran y maldicen en su lengua los niños.

Pero nadie les roba
el candor de las primeras aguas de la madre.

Así nacieron.

The Children of the Rain

All day I hear the noise of waters
Making moan.
—James Joyce

The children of the rain ascend and descend along
the silvery seam the moon stitches in the hills.

The children of the rain are the grandchildren
of a mestiza grandmother who stayed behind to die
in houses built of larch trees bordering the lake.
The children know how to step through the swamps like
blind horses. But at the slightest misstep
they turn into arrows
        or ghostly dwarves.

The children of the rain
        are more surrealistic than Breton,
more ancient and more childlike than Huidobro:
        I wonder again, Is it because they were going to be mute
        that God gave them those eyes?
The children of the rain are neither bad nor good
they swear and curse in their language, the children do.

But no one robs them of
the purity of their mothers' first waters.

That is how they were born.

Aunque lea y escriba

Aunque lea y escriba
el animal que hay en mi guarda
me enseña a interpretar la maldición del búho
más allá de todas las palabras.

Me enseña a tener visiones que no son
            visiones sino anunciamientos
tocados en la sombra
para ordenar los huesos en su alma
me enseña.

Aunque lea y escriba
veo en las nubes del poniente
            un teatro fantasma
en el escenario mítico de Quenteyao,
el que ordena quien aparece o desaparece,
entre los alerzales de San Juan de la Costa.

Aunque lea y escriba
y pase por letrada, no puedo desnegar la ubre
que espesa las natas de mis presentimientos

sin más agarradura que
las señas secretas palpadas en la muda matriz
del universo.

Although I May Read and Write

Although I may read and write
the animal that's under my care
teaches me to interpret the owl's curse
that goes beyond all words.

He teaches me to have visions that aren't
          visions but annunciations
sensed in the shadows
to arrange the bones in his soul
he teaches me.

Although I may read and write
I see in the clouds of the setting sun
          a ghostly theater
on the mythic stage of Wuenteyao,
the one who orders appearances and disappearances
among the larch groves of San Juan de la Costa.

Although I may read and write
and pass for a learned woman, I cannot deny the udder
that curdles the cream of my premonitions

without more grasping than
the secret signs, felt in the mute womb
of the universe.

Salmón de río

Y espíritu del río, espíritu del mar
no permitas que me aleje
deja que mi plegaria te alcance.
—T.S. Eliot

Usted, que es afuerino, ¿ha visto
subir el salmón contra la corriente, ha visto
la transparencia de los ríos de Chile
donde las pancoras escriben en piedra
la carta astral de los vivientes?

Usted, que es afuerino, ¿ha sentido
la queja de la Santa
ahogada en las pozas sin fondo
como en las pozas de las que dan a luz
        goteando
hasta la rotura de su bolsa?

Usted, que es afuerino, debe aprender
        el decálogo de la abuelas huilliches
orilleras durante 300 años,
        de las vegas pastosas
que no se salvaron del diluvio.

Usted, que es afuerino, ¿tendría pulmones
para remontar el mismo río en que su madre
abrió las piernas para darle vida?

River Salmon

And spirit of the river, spirit of the sea,
Suffer me not to be separated
And let my cry come unto thee.
—T.S. Eliot, "Ash Wednesday"

You, outsider, have you seen
the salmon swimming against the current, have you seen
the transparency of Chilean rivers
where crayfish write on stone
the astral chart of the living?

You, outsider, have you sensed
the complaint of the Saint
drowned in bottomless wells
as in the wells of women who give birth
         dripping
until the rupture of their sac?

You, outsider, must learn
         the decalogue of Huilliche grandmothers,
shoreline algae gatherers for 300 years,
         of the thick, low swampground
that wasn't saved from the flood.

You, outsider, would you possibly have the lungs
to swim upstream in the same river where your mother
opened her legs to give you life?

Huelga de brazos caídos

Como si la hazaña
no consistiera en ser
vulnerable.
—M. Yourcenar

Hoy no quiero sentirme vulnerable.
Hoy no escribo. Me forro el talón de Aquiles
y todos los talones con calcetín de yeso.

Prefiero salir con mis perros a rastrear
la huella del zorro-chingue.
Para eso tengo olfato y oído de tísica.

Hoy no quiero ser blanco de nadie.
¿Oyeron? Tampoco iré al jardín con
Rainer Maria Rilke las espinas pueden ser
traicioneras y, menos le pediré
a don Sigmund que me tire las cartas del psicoanálisis.

No estoy para hazañas. Hoy no escribo.
Me declaro en huelga señoras y señores.

Strike of Lowered Arms

As if the great achievement
did not consist of being
vulnerable.
—M. Yourcenar

Today I don't want to feel vulnerable.
Today I won't write. I cover my Achilles heel
and every heel with a plaster cast.

I prefer to go out with my dogs to track
footprints of the skunk.
For that I have the sense of smell and hearing of a consumptive.

Today I don't wish to be anyone's target.
Did you hear me? Nor will I go to the garden with
Rainer Maria Rilke the thorns may be
treacherous, and least of all will I ask
Sigmund to read the cards of psychoanalysis for me.

I'm not in the mood for great deeds. Today I won't write.
I declare myself on strike ladies and gentlemen.

El día que murió el Tony Caluga

Todo lo que la infancia
acoge, tiene una virtud
de origen
—G. Bachelard

El día que murió Caluga, la Santa
lloró sobre los campos de alfalfa,

los niños gritaron: ¡*Hoy nadie muere aquí!*
      y el eco de
los montes. . .*muere aquíííííí!*
Entonces tragaron un espejo
para fijar la imagen de la carpa de infancia
cuando el mundo era un círculo
estacado por los duendes del bosque.

¡*Hoy nadie muere aquí!*
      repitieron los niños
y con las manos embarradas
trancaron el portón de los patios de entierro.

Sólo el Telón de Boca quedó abierto
por si acaso.

The Day Tony Caluga Died

*All that childhood
shelters has the virtue
of beginnings*
—G. Bachelard

The day Caluga died, the Saint
sobbed over the fields of alfalfa,

the children shouted, *Today no one will die here!*
     And the echo from
the hills... *die heeeere.*
Then they swallowed a mirror
to capture the image of childhood's tent
when the world was a circle
surrounded by the spirits of the woods.

Today no one will die here!
     repeated the children
and with their mud-smeared hands
they barred the gate of the burial grounds.

Only the Final Curtain remained open
just in case.

La última llorona

Rezando a gritos
para oír si rezaba.
—Juan Rulfo

Vicky Báez ¿cómo se llora sin ti, ahora
que agarraste altura hacia el firmamento
sin dejar alumnas ni instrucciones precisas
en lo tocante a velorios de pobre,
   de angelitos sentados?
Las guitarras, Vicky, están desafinadas
sin encordado para el amor de Dios
en su estribillo, asentadas las vocales
sin tu aire. Muda la casa.

¿Cómo se llora con decencia
o se dice el responso
que alimpia las quemas del pecado?
¿Dónde fuiste a leer tus propias Sagradas
   Escrituras
para saber en qué momento
comenzó a correr tu eternidad de arriba?

Mientras yo, desde abajo, por lo comido
   y lo rezado
en los entierros del campo, te declaro:
la más antigua reina de los llantos.

The Last Weeping Woman

Vicky Báez, how can we cry without you, now
that you've grabbed hold of the sky
without leaving students or precise instructions
with regard to the wakes of the poor,
the little seated angels?
The guitars, Vicky, are out of tune
without strings for God's love
in their refrain, the words settled down
without your air. The house mute.

How does one cry with decency
or provide the response
that purifies the fires of sin?
Where did you go to read your own Sacred
Writings
to know at what moment
your eternity above began to run its course?

While I, down below, by what was eaten
        and what was prayed
in the funerals of the countryside, declare you:

the most ancient queen of lamentations.

Básica

Sin decir esta boca es mía
yo digo: esta boca es mía,

porque la tierra hace hablar sin habla.

Basic

Without saying a word
I say: this is my word,

because the earth creates speech without speaking.

Comala & Tacamó S.A.

¿Está seguro de que ya es Comala?
Seguro, señor.
-¿Y por qué se ve esto tan triste?
Son los tiempos, señor.
—Juan Rulfo

Y yo aquí, sentadita entre Comala y Tacamó,
apuntalando
estrellas fronterizas que no son fronterizas,
porque en el cabo del mundo
no hay límites, ni separación de bienes.
Todo es una Patagonia y da lo mismo,
que la tierra esté arriba y los cielos abajo.

Y yo aquí, entre las vacas y las yeguas,
para leer la suerte en el ojo de la ventolera
que desveló mi infancia.

Por eso, sigo en mi condición geográfica:
una lejura silenciosa
una fiebre pegada entre las sienes
por encontrar los seres idos
       en este mismo mundo,
como si todo fuera un solo mundo.

Entonces, Comala y Tacamó,
corresponden a la misma envoltura
por fundamentos mágicos.

¿O será puramente la tristeza
de los tiempos que corren, don J. Rulfo?

Comala & Tacamó, S.A.

Are you sure we have reached Comala?
Absolutely, sir.
And why does it all look so sad?
It's the times, sir.
—Juan Rulfo

And here I am, seated between Comala and Tacamó,
shoring up
border stars that are not borders,
because at the tip of the world
there are no limits, nor separation of goods.
It is all Patagonia and it makes no difference
that the earth is above and the heavens below.

And here I am, between the cows and the mares,
to read my fortune in the eye of the gust of wind
that disturbed my childhood sleep.

Therefore, I persist in my geographic condition:
a silent distant place
a fever stuck between my temples
to find departed beings
          in this very world,
as if everything were a single world.

Then, Comala and Tacamó
correspond to the same envelope
through magical fundamentals.

Or is it simply the sadness
of the passing times Mr. J. Rulfo?

Cuestión de vida o muerte

Aquellos que vivieron antes que yo,
que a veces se disuelven
urdieron lo que soy.
—Rainer Maria Rilke

En el sur
los muertos no se entierran,
se disuelven en la niebla.

Así el Dios de la barba de palo
hace el pase mágico y el cuerpo pasa a
          nube, o
a fantasma sin guión dramático.

Sucede que hoy, no se ven ni las manos
en la sopera helada de la tierra, por eso,
los del Paralelo 40 Sur
andamos como pisando huevos
          en los pastos vidriosos
de las vegas de Chile.

Andamos valientes sin saber, si hoy
todo sera cuestión de vida o muerte.

Question of Life or Death

Those who lived before me,
who sometimes dissolve,
plotted what I am.
—Rainer Maria Rilke

In the South
the dead aren't buried,
they dissolve in the mist.

Thus the God with the wooden beard
performs a magical gesture and the body becomes
        a cloud, or
a ghost without a dramatic script.

It happens that today not even our hands are seen
in the frozen soup bowl of the earth, therefore,
those of us living south of the 40th parallel
walk as if stepping on eggs
        in the glassy pastures
of damp Chilean lowlands.

We walk bravely not knowing if today
it will all be a question of life or death.

Examen de conciencia

La conciencia si se oye,
        pasa a ser conciencia,
pero, si no se oye
        nadie reclama de su inconsciencia.

Y yo, poco es lo que oigo.

Amén.

Examination of Conscience

Conscience if it's heard,
      becomes consciousness,
but, if it's not heard,
      no one puts in a claim for his lack of conscience.

And me, what I hear is very little.

Amen.

¿Cómo es la cosa?

La cosa es: sin perder la inocencia,
quedarse cruda como pájara silvestre
en estado de empollamiento
      (o de tentación),
siempre lúcida, lúcida.   Esa es la cosa.

Pero, la cosa, también es salvarse
      de un modo emocional,
jamás cerebro-vascular.

No tener miedo es la clave.

Nada peor que atornillarse a las vigas de la
      memoria:
aquella es una geometría especial
      que nunca ordenaremos.

La cosa es salir del huevo y
saber a qué lado amanece
      por si volviéramos a nacer.

Esa es la cosa.

What's the Thing?

The thing is: without losing one's innocence,
to remain uncivilized like a wild bird
in a state of breeding
        (or temptation),
always lucid, lucid That's the thing.

But the thing is also to save one's self
        in an emotional way,
never cerebro-vascular.

Not to be afraid is the key.
Nothing worse than screwing oneself to the rafters of
        memory:
That is a spatial geometry
        we shall never put in order.

The thing is to emerge from the egg and
know on which side it dawns
        in case we're born again.

That's the thing.

Espacio Mahler

A Juan Pablo Izquierdo

Aquí en el sur del mundo, donde el
silencio de los vivos
constituye un cuerpo con el silencio
de los muertos
y todo es una nave de catedral vacía,
un rezo,
en la sinfónica percusíon del viento,

aquí en el sur
me cruza Mahler, Carl Gustav Mahler, en
los cuatro sentidos cardinales
donde el espacio es una respiración de las
lenguas antárticas
un frío redentor, libre, como un cóndor
de alturas.

Aquí en el sur se marca con bautizo:
una pila escarchada de la que nadie huye
no hay puertas de entrada ni salida

solo la música   la música.

Mahler Space

To Juan Pablo Izquierdo

Here in the southernmost part of the world, where the
silence of the living
forms a body with the silence
of the dead
and everything is an empty cathedral nave,
a prayer,
in the symphonic percussion of the wind,

here in the south
Mahler passes through me. Carl Gustav Mahler, in
the four cardinal directions
where space is a breath from
antarctic tongues
a redeeming cold, free like a condor
on high.

Here in the south one is marked by baptism:
a frozen font from which no one flees
there are no doors for entering or leaving

only music, music.

Se pasa llave a la chapa de 1931

Con el silencio se barren las pisadas
pero no la memoria. Cuando naces
el tema de la vida y de la muerte
            hacen palpable
al hijo, la partera te zurce
            el cuerpo físico,
las potencias, pero ¿quién garantiza
            una definición de tu alma?

Y comienza la marcha de regreso.
La mudez necesaria en su rigor interno
es lo que más importa,   solas
            caen las máscaras.

La dimensión de origen no se altera:
Dios quiso que respires tu metro cúbico
            de aire
y que un día...no fuera.

Por eso hay una hora en que llega la hora de
pasar cerrojo a las chapas de infancia.
(Un fierro martillado de los mil novecientos.)

Decir adiós con las luces encendidas
podría ser una oración valiente.

Locking the Door on 1931

With silence footsteps are erased
but not memory. When you're born
the theme of life and death
makes the child
palpable, the midwife mends
your physical body,
your potential, but who guarantees
        a definition of your soul?

And the march of return begins.
The silence necessary in its internal rigor
is what matters most, alone
        the masks fall.

The dimension of origin is not altered:
God willed you to breathe your cubic meter
        of air
and one day...it will not be.

For that reason there comes a time
for bolting the locks on the doors of childhood.
(Iron hammered in the nineteen hundreds.)

Saying goodbye with the lights on
could be a brave statement.

Mi abuela tocaba el piano con sombrero

La anciana concertista exigía silencio,
orejas limpias y castidad de pensamientos
en los huecos sensuales del cerebro.

La anciana tocaba el piano con sombrero
para enjaular el vuelo de las notas
desvanecidas en el entierro de los siglos,

y nosotros, los ladrones de nidos, sentados
                a la fuerza
con las uñas comidas, siempre
                temiendo al viento,
a los crujidos de las piezas cerradas
donde solo entraban los grandes y los
muertos.

Eso era todo.
El olor a alcanfor en las sillas
de Viena,
un estado de invención   de magia
para fijar a fuego la música heredada
en las cajas de canto:
una sonata de aguas el piano
sin necesidad de las palabras.

> *Todavía*
> *los ladrones de nidos*
> *usamos*
> *poco*
> *las palabras.*

My Grandmother Played the Piano with her Hat On

The elderly concert artist demanded silence,
clean ears and chaste thoughts
in the sensual cavities of the brain.

The old woman played the piano with her hat on
to cage the flight of notes
vanished in the burial of centuries,

and we, the robbers of nests, seated
          by force
with our nails chewed, always
          fearing the wind
and the creaking from closed rooms
where only adults and the
dead entered.

That was all.
The smell of camphor in the chairs
from Vienna,
a state of invention of magic
to firmly fasten the music inherited
in the music boxes:
a sonata of waters the piano
with no need for words.

We
robbers of nests
still use
words
sparingly.

Salgo a penar en las colinas

Nació de nube sin derecho a madre, dijo la partera,
eso dijo, y yo, insegura de mundo
asomada-animal con mis respiros.

No sé si nació viva o está inventando, dijo la partera,
pero si pasa a existencial será mágica,
para eso le amarro el ombligo con alambre, dijo.

Mientras arriba de la casa, esa mancha vidriosa,
el ojo de agua como empezando un llanto
que duraría siempre, y más arriba
la bandada de gansos salvajes cortaba el círculo
del cielo.

Así aprendí la anatomía humana, la desdoblada
entre este mundo y otro para arropar mi alma.

Así aprendí a penar sin tener pena, sin morir
en la danza perpetua de los muertos.

Pero nació de nube sin derecho a madre, repitió la partera
tal vez para asustarme, yo la eschuché clarita
con mis propios oídos
y la sigo escuchando cuando salgo a penar en las colinas
y trajino avidada por las claves mayores:

> "Dios no quiere que tú tengas
> sol, si conmigo no marchas."

I Go Out to Grieve in the Hills

She was born from a cloud without the right to a mother,
said the midwife, she said that, and I, insecure about the world
animal-like with my breaths.

I don't know if she was born alive or is invented, the midwife said,
but if she passes into existence, she'll be magical,
so I'll tie her navel with wire, she said.

While above the house, that glassy stain,
the eye of water, as if beginning a lament
that would last forever, and even higher
a flock of wild geese cut a circle
in the sky.

Thus I learned human anatomy, split open
between this world and another to dress my soul.

Thus I learned to suffer without pain, without dying
in the perpetual dance of the dead.

But she was born from a cloud without the right to a mother,
repeated the midwife
perhaps to frighten me, I heard her clearly
with my own ears
and I still hear her when I go out to grieve in the hills
and I hustle and bustle, warned by the major keys:

> "God doesn't want you to have
> sun, if you do not accompany me."

Con las claves a salvo
soy digna de la nube y de la madre
¿o no, Gabriela?

With the keys safe
I'm worthy of the cloud and the mother,
aren't I, Gabriela?

Entra por un oído, sale por el otro

Dice la vieja:hablo por experiencia.
Entra por un oído, sale por el otro.

De pie señores: ¡la frase para el bronce!
Entra por un oído, sale por el otro.

La jura de amor eterno...
Entra por un oído, sale por el otro.

Sigue la vieja, sigo: las vírgenes no pueden
bailar con los finados, porque todo se pega
como la tos de perro.
Entra por un oído, sale por el otro.

El graznido del Caiquén en la noche
acalambra la mente
y puede paralizar tu sombra.
Entra por un oído, sale por el otro.

El miedo, el silbido del Diablo,
la cumbia y el rock del milenio,
entran por un oído, salen por el otro.

Pero morir entra por un oído
                    y
                    no
                    sale.

It Goes in One Ear and Out the Other

The old woman says: I speak from experience.
It goes in one ear and out the other.

Attention gentlemen: the phrase for the bronze!
It goes in one ear and out the other.

The vow of eternal love...
It goes in one ear and out the other.

The old woman continues, I continue: virgins cannot
dance with the dead, because everything is contagious
like a doggone cough.
It goes in one ear and out the other.

The cackling of geese in the night
cramps the mind
and can paralyze your shadow.
It goes in one ear and out the other.

Fear, the devil's whistle,
cumbia and millennial rock,
go in one ear and out the other.

But dying goes in one ear

        and
        does not
        come out.

Oración clase B

Óyeme Cristo-Jesús: no quiero ser viva enterrada
por la ley del hombre ni espectadora de la primera fila,

prefiero municiones reventando mis pechos
y una tabla verde para escribir del sol-de-agua
que reveló esta mezcla de pasión
gatillando entre el valor y el miedo.

Óyeme , pues Jesús, la revoltura de maldades
que rastrillan mi alma como a cualquier mujer
viviente y deslenguada, suelta de cuerpo al aire libre.

       Óyeme, J.H.S.
       Sería todo por ahora.
       Amén

Class B Prayer

Hear me, Jesus Christ: I don't want to be buried alive
by man's law or a spectator in the first row,

I prefer munitions bursting my breasts
and a green tablet on which to write about the rain-predicting sun
that revealed this mix of passion
pulling the trigger between courage and fear.

Hear me, then, Jesus, the mixture of evils
that rake my soul like any woman
living and shameless, freed from her body into the open air.

> Hear me, Lord Jesus.
> That will be all for now.
> Amen.

Réquiem porque murió la Rita
(poema con posdata)

Pero no la Hayworth ni la etiquetada Tres Medallas,
Tampoco la de Casia abogada de los imposibles.

Esta es, la que gritó en Misa de Doce:

> "yo soy humilde y, tú ¿eres humilde?
> ¿Quién es humilde aquíííííí?..."

la que provocó parálisis de lengua
y silencios perpetuos.

La Rita mía, crecío sin garantía en los caminos,
loca y valiente como perra de circo.
dejó cartas tiradas en la mesa de los pájaros
que no tenían mesa
y le escribía a Dios sin firma, la Rita.

Hoy, por tercera boca,
supe que "murió de ausencia"
en un siquiátrico de Santiago muda de amor
cuando manos piadosas
la sacaron de su estado de cabeza
para que nunca más cortara el Evangelio de golpe
con preguntas indecentes.

Así murió la Rita. Sin fecha. Como sombra.

Requiem for the Death of Rita
(poem with postscript)

But not Hayworth or labeled Tres Medallas,
or Saint Rita, advocate of impossibilities.

It's this one, the one who shouted at Midnight Mass:

> "I'm humble, and you, are you humble?
> Who is humble heeeere?..."

the one who provoked paralysis of the tongue
and perpetual silences.

My Rita grew up without a guarantee in the streets,
crazy and brave as a circus dog.
She left cards tossed on the table of birds
that did not have a table
and wrote to God without a signature, Rita.

Today, from a rumor all over town,
I learned she "died of longing"
in a psychiatric hospital in Santiago mute with love
when pious hands
relieved her of her state of mind
so that never again would she suddenly interrupt the Gospel
with indecent questions.

That's how Rita died. Unknown date. Like a shadow.

* Posdata.

Rita, por favor no descanses en paz. Sigue preguntando
desde arriba. ¿quién es humilde aquí?...a lo mejor,
algunos duros podrían responderte, entonces pasarías
de loca a milagrera. ¿Qué te parece Rita de Corales?
No descanses, aunque sea en homenaje al circo.

*Postscript
    Rita, please don't rest in peace. Continue asking
    from above, Who's humble here?... Perhaps,
    some harsh people might answer you, then you would change
    from madwoman to miracle-worker. What do you think Rita
    of Corales?
    Don't rest, even though it may be in homage to the circus.

Poema de autor

Somos libres. Tu beso es mi rehén,
la valentía que nunca se arrodilla.

Mas, líbranos Señor de todo mal. Así sea.

Author's Poem

We're free. Your kiss is my hostage,
courage that never kneels.

But, free us Lord from all evil. Amen.

Volvió el diluvio

Volvió pero sin Arca de Noé,
sin paloma ponedora, ni olivo. Volvió
como imitación de anillo enchapado en oro
con luces de artificio para pantalla grande y
el registro histórico para la TV cable.

Volvió como nacido de aguas muertas:
cada uno en lo suyo, trepando
como si la inmortalidad o la grandeza
dependieran del peso en los bolsillos,
del orgullo de casta, de coronas compradas.

Volvió, cuando nadie reza ni besa.

Volvió el Diluvio, hijo mío. Y yo
soy la Isabel de García Márquez
"viendo llover en Macondo".

Return of the Flood

It returned but without Noah's Ark,
without a laying dove or an olive branch. It returned
like an imitation gold-plated ring
with artificial lighting for the wide screen and
the historical record for cable TV.

It returned as if born from dead waters:
each one on its own, climbing
as if immortality or greatness
depended on the weight in one's pockets,
on the pride of race, on purchased crowns.

It returned, when no one prays or kisses.

The Flood returned, my child. And I
am García Márquez's Isabel
"watching it rain in Macondo."

El amor animal de las cachorras

Las cachorras de mi perra-loba
huelen a leche ácida a tentación de teta tibia,
las cachorras.

Son encarnaciones que anconcharon
los sueños de la luz y de la sombra
en la desembocadura de la infancia.
Perras huachas, paridas con miedo al fondo
de bodegas abandonadas donde la historia
es escritura hablada
raspando la quebrazón de la memoria.

Eso es todo. El amor animal de las cachorras
no exige ley civil ni religiosa, está siempre
entre el hocico húmedo y mi alma.

The Animal Love of Puppies

The puppies of my wolf-dog
smell of sour milk, the temptation of tepid teats,
the puppies.

They're incarnations that sustained
dreams of light and shadow
in the outflowing of childhood.
Bastard dogs given birth fearfully in the back
of abandoned warehouses where history
is spoken writing
scratching the rupture of memory.

That's all. The animal love of puppies
doesn't demand civil or religious law, it's present always
between their moist mouths and my soul.

Datos confidenciales

"Escuchémosla hablar, roto
el silencio no atinaremos a
llamarla ausente."
—Enrique Lihn

Igual que la humareda (roto el silencio)
entró al sueño circular la Vicky Báez,
sin firmar papeles ni conocer la ficha clínica,
sin soltar su alma la Vicky.

En su hoja de vida — estrictamente conversada —
dejó dicho que morir callada era pecado
que se iba tranquila pero que no se iba,
que dejaba a sus herederas en la manga,
amaestradas para que el arte de sacra maldición
jurada, no quedara en el aire como el "Clavel del Aire"
porque en ese aire podrían filtrarse
los que siempre cortaron la leche con
su mala leche.

Y yo, encargada de los humos y las velas
sé muy bien, quienes son las valientes, las que
desordenan el rebaño con salidas de madre,
dignos hijas de Brecht y del coraje.

El resto, viene a ser confidencial. Me pertenece.

Confidential Data

*"Let us listen to her speak, the silence
broken, we shall not hit the mark by
declaring her absent."*
—Enrique Lihn

Just like incense (the silence broken)
Vicky Baez entered the circular dream,
without signing papers or knowing her medical profile,
without releasing her soul Vicky.

In her curriculum vita—strictly spoken—
she let it be said that dying silently was a sin
that she was leaving calmly but she was not leaving,
she was leaving her heirs little money,
trained so the sworn art of sacred swearing
would not remain in the air like the "Clavel del Aire"
because into that air might filter
those who always soured the milk with
their sour grapes.

And I, in charge of incense and candles
know very well who the valiant women are, those who
upset the apple-cart by losing control
worthy daughters of Brecht and courage.

The rest turns out to be confidential. It belongs to me.

Molino de agua

El agua madre baja de los montes
a la rueda de palo atornillada en la memoria.

Es el molino marcando el paso de la niebla
que confunde los años y los daños,
el catecismo goteado en la mitad de la cabeza
para crecer, decían, como Dios manda,
como el Cristo-Dios clavado, decían,
como la eternidad que rije las buenas y las malas
en la aspas del molino que hice a mano
con el consentimiento de los ancianos muertos,
cuando me parieron sobre un pañal de crea cruda
sin palabras heroicas.

En la rueda de palo va a girar la conciencia
hasta que el agua madre muere seca.

(gracias mi Dios, por la LUZ que me hace ver.)

Waterwheel

The mother water descends from the mountains
to the wooden wheel screwed to memory.

It is the mill marking the passage of mist
that confounds years and injuries,
the catechism dripped into the center of one's head
to grow, they said, as God commands,
like the nailed Christ-God, they said,
like the eternity that rules good and evil
in the blades of the mill I built by hand
with the consent of the elderly dead,
when they gave birth to me on a cloth of rough cotton
without heroic words.

On the wooden wheel consciousness will spin
until the mother water dies dried-up.

(thank you, my God, for the LIGHT that lets me see.)

Apuntes

El poeta no tiene cielos concretos,
muere siempre sin acabo de sueños.

Muere como artificio del mito,
parte y reparte su inocencia
que es facultad humana y facultad de bestia

pero no muere.

Notes

The poet doesn't have concrete heavens,
he always dies without the death of dreams.

He dies as the artifice of myth,
splits and shares his innocence
that is a human attribute and a bestial attribute

but he doesn't die.

Mentadas americanas

Introducción

Mientras Frida Kahlo mira a través del vidrio, fajada en cuero-
claveteado por su "Columna Rota" (México 1944), las mujeres del
silencio americano, pintan su historia sin marco—sin marco—en
las telas raspadas del viento.

Primera estrofa

Aquí, la María-Vitoca pedaleando en la bicicleta
que le cayó del cielo. Entre chupada y chupada
de Belmont King Size, hace de catequista
en la Sede Social de la aldea.
Tiene palabra grande y no sabe leer. Predica
composturas de alma y chamuscados del infierno
con fervor de anima santa.

Ella es mi catecismo, modestamente hablando.

La María-Vitoca jura y rejura sobre la tumba de su madre
que rezar no es lo mismo que fumar
que nadie puede zapatear sobre el bien y el mal
—hay que aclarar las cosas—dice, mientras
se pinta los ojos y se hace la permanente
aún sabiendo que nada es permanente.

Famous American Women

While Frida Kahlo looks through the window, girdled in studded
leather for her "Broken Column" (Mexico, 1944), the women of
American silence paint their unframed story—without a frame—
on the scratchy canvasses of the wind.

First stanza

Here, Maria-Vitoca pedaling the bicycle
that fell on her from the sky. Between taking drags
on King Size Belmonts, she acts as catechist
in the village social hall.
She uses big words and doesn't know how to read. She preaches
sedateness of soul and the scorching of Hell
with the fervor of a saintly soul.

She is my catechism, modestly speaking.

Maria-Vitoca affirms and reaffirms on her mother's grave
that praying is not the same as smoking
that no one can tap-dance over good and evil
—things must be made clear—she says, while
she makes up her eyes and acts like she's here to stay
even knowing that nothing lasts forever.

Segunda estrofa

La Sra. Yike Maldonado cerró la venta de huevos
en su gallinero de invierno. Razón de sabiduría:
    "Las gallinas no ponen, están inconclusas,
    secas de yema, porque el gallo anda concentrado
    por otros corrales de Dios."

Tercera estrofa

Ana Torres, florista en la esquina del viento,
después de cincuenta años, pasó a ser Ana Fuentes,
en su mismo kiosko y con el mismo viento.
Sucede que ayer se tiñó rubio el pelo
para espantar los malos sueños que en sueños
le enterraron al hijo, sin preparación ni agua de arrenta.

Y entre begonias y azaleas (cada flor es un estado de alma)
no sabe la Ana si sentirse Torres o sentirse Fuentes
en la misma esquina del otro viejo viento,
porque aprendió a hablar sola, sin contestación presente.

Pero, ella sabe que los nombres no salvan.

Postdata.
Yo acuso el golpe, mientras Frida Kahlo con su "Columna Rota,"
México 1944, mira a través de un vidrio empavonado lo que sus
mujeres de América escriben sin saber leer ni escribir.

Second stanza

Mrs. Yike Maldonado stopped the sale of eggs
in her winter henhouse. Reasoning from knowledge:
   "The hens aren't laying, their eggs are immature,
   with dried-up yolks, because the cock wanders focused
   on God's other barnyards."

Third stanza

Ana Torres, florist on the windy corner,
after fifty years, became Ana Fuentes,
in her same kiosk and with the same wind.
It happens that yesterday she bleached her hair blond
to frighten away bad dreams because in dreams
they buried her son, without preparation or mint water.

And between begonias and azaleas (each flower a state of the soul)
Ana does not know whether to feel like a Torres or a Fuentes
on the same corner of another old wind,
because she learned to talk to herself, without any response.

   But she knows that names don't bring salvation.

Postscript
I feel the effect, while Frida Kahlo with her "Broken Column."
Mexico 1944, looks through a blurry window at what her women
of America write without knowing how to read or write.

C.I. 3.036.331-0

Soy la que a ratos le resucita la mente
y adivina los cuadernos del porvenir que es
un invento del pasado muerto y sepultado.

Soy la que vive en los pantanos del sur,
la que no necesita guardaespaldas
contra las esquirlas que, de pronto, revientan el
sistema planetario de la ordenación celeste,
para resacar el poder de Dios
contra el poder del hombre.

Yo la 3.036.331-0, inscrita en el Civil
no sé si a tiempo o a destiempo, registrada
en el libro de la niebla   porque nunca
apareció la sílaba de mi salvación y nunca
volvió la misma niebla y la niña de pecho
pasó a ser hija de una mujer muerta
en las canteras tramposas de la noche
sin reloj de pared sin ficha personal
ni celebramientos, ni nada.

Sólo el agua empozada en la amarradura del
ombligo, donde cuajan las sales de Chile.

Yo, número tanto y tanto, ¡qué importa!
a estas alturas de muñeca pintada, de pobrecita
que enterró su espejo para siempre
a sabiendas que el cuadro de honor
no es lo mismo que el cuadro de horror,

ID 3.036.331-0

I'm the one whose mind is sometimes resuscitated
and who divines the notebooks of the future which is
an invention of the dead and buried past.

I 'm the one who lives in the southern swamps
the one who doesn't need a bodyguard
for the splinters which suddenly blow up the
planetary system of heavenly order,
to recapture the power of God
against the power of man.

I number 3.036.331-0, inscribed in the Registry
either on time or at the wrong time, registered
in the book of mist because never
did a word for my salvation appear and never
did the same mist return and the child at my breast
became the daughter of a dead woman
in the uneven hollows of the night
without a clock on the wall without an ID card
or celebrations, or anything.

Only the water submerged in the tying of the
umbilical cord, where the salts of Chile curdle.

I, number such-and-such, what does it matter!
At this stage of being a painted doll, a poor little thing
who buried her mirror forever
knowing full well that a portrait of honor
is not the same as a portrait of horror,

a sabiendas que esta fragilidad sin vuelta
confunde el razonamiento con el entendimiento.
A sabiendas.

Entonces ¿quién será la 3.036.331-0?

knowing full well this fragility without return
confuses reasoning with understanding.
Knowing.

Then who can number 3.036.331-0 be?

Retrato de una mujer

Estaba
más triste que la tierra encima de un muerto.

Lucía pechos secos y un relámpago encostrado
en sus cuencas de mujer lastimada
por la salmuera de los riscos andinos, donde
ningún libro tenía letras, ni amor.

Y, bueno, tampoco podría decirse que
alguna vez, en su puntuda vida-puta,

ella
tuvo libros
con letras
de amor.

Portrait of a woman

She was
sadder than the dirt covering a corpse.

She revealed dried-up breasts and a lightning bolt
encrusted in her eye sockets, a woman wounded
by the salty brine of Andean cliffs where
no book contained letters, or love.

And, well, neither could you say that
at some point in her jagged bitch of a life,

she
received books
with letters
of love.

La voz cortada

*"Y ya que a ti no llega mi voz ruda,
óyeme sordo, pues me quejo muda."*
—Sor Juana Inés de la Cruz

Vamos
en nombre del animal que nos habita,
de martillos que clavan la noche
a un beso ciego,

vamos
con las voces cortadas por un espejo roto
a rescatar de nuevo los dones del silencio,

vamos callando
agarrados al hueco de la mano de Cristo.

Severed Voice

Let's go
in the name of the animal that inhabits us,
of hammers that split the night
at a blind kiss,

let's go
with voices severed by a broken mirror
to rescue once more the gifts of silence,

let's go silently
grasping the hollow of Christ's hand.

Mapa de infancia

*"El regreso se hace
entre los perros del miedo"*
—M. Yourcenar

Nadie sabe cuando empieza el regreso.
Los viajes son cuerpos desvanecidos
en las camisetas de la niebla.

La leyenda del niño
es una alquimia de luz sobre los vidrios.
Su monólogo oscila entre el valor y el miedo
cuando aullan los perros en creciente
acompañando la oración de un muerto.

Su mapa es la memoria no fechada en los libros.

Un trazado invisible
siempre marca la vuelta hacia el ombligo
de una mujer que huele a leche ácida desde
la fundación del tiempo.

Map of Childhood

"The return takes place
among the dogs of fear"
—M. Yourcenar

No one knows when the return begins.
Journeys are bodies dissipated
in shirts of mist.

The legend of the child
is an alchemy of light on the windows.
His monologue fluctuates between bravery and fear
when dogs howl at the crescent moon
accompanying the prayer of a corpse.

His map is dateless memory in books.

An invisible tracery
always marks the return to the navel
of a woman who's smelled of sour milk since
the beginning of time.

Descubrimientos

Los amerindios descubrieron el sol.
Los yaganes, el centro de la lluvia.
Los letrados, el altar de su propia cabeza.

Y yo, que no soy amerindia, letrada ni yagana,
declaro mi total descubrimiento:

este corazón
lobo-rabioso
que me aulla a morir.

Discoveries

Amerindians discovered the sun.
The Yaganes, the heart of rain.
The learned, the altar of their own heads.

And I, neither Amerindian, learned nor Yagán,
declare my entire discovery:

this rabid-wolf
heart
that howls at me to die.

Lápiz de leche

No importa que me entierren o desentierren
al pie de los volcanos. Da lo mismo.

Nací de avenas huachas de sangres idas y venidas
entre las costas del Báltico y la Butuhuillimapu
del paralelo 40 sur.

Allí se mestizaron las sangres y sus crías.

Sobrevivo: maleza en los patios de sombra,
y vengo a ser guardiana de Icoquih
—la estrella que aparece antes del sol—según el *Popol Vuh,*
y vengo a ser guardiana de una modesta historia
escrita con "lápiz de leche"
en la levedad de las nieves de infancia.

Que me entierren o desentierren da lo mismo.
No hay boleta de garantía para la eternidad.

Pero están volcanes.

Stick of Chalk

It doesn't matter if they inter me or disinter me
at the foot of the volcanoes. It's all the same.

I was born of bastard pastoral pipes of bloodlines ebbing and
flowing
between the coasts of the Baltic and the Butahuillimapu
on the 40th parallel south.

There blood and seed were mixed.

I survive: thicket in the patios of shadow,
And I become the guardian of Icoquih
—the star that appears before the sun—according to the *Popol
        Vuh,*
and I become the guardian of a modest history
written with a stick of chalk
in the lightness of childhood snowfalls.

Let them inter me or disinter me it's all the same.
There is no guaranteed ticket for eternity.

But volcanoes exist.

Cuajos del frío

"Ninguna nevada pudo morderme.
Hielos punzantes sobre mi alma."
—Emily Dickinson

Las jaleas recién cuajadas de la clorofila
multiplican el verde-oscuro de estos bosques
que vienen a ser tus cosas y las mías.

Tiempo vertical crucificado pero no santificado
en esta punta americana,
en estos sistemas planetarios escarchados sobre el polo sur,
sin registro en las astronomías del XXI.

Estas son nuestras cosas, Dickinson, sin pulido de verbo,
ni artificios
sin Legiones de Honor en los dos pechos.

Y todo a sangre fría. Aunque un poco mordidas, reconozco.

Curdling from the Cold

> "Not a sleet could bite me—
> Icicles upon my soul."
> —Emily Dickinson

The recently curdled preserves of chlorophyll
multiply the dark green of these forests
that become your things and mine.

Vertical time crucified but not sanctified
in this American point,
in these hoarfrosted planetary systems above the South Pole,
unrecorded in the astronomies of the twenty-first century.

These things are ours, Dickinson, without polished word,
or finesse
without Legions of Honor on both our breasts.

And all in cold blood. Although slightly bitten, I realize.

La ruda
(Ruta graveoleus)

La Ruda combate la anudación de nervios,
el vacío de alma y el vacío de estómago,
pero, sobre todo, sus hojas quemadas
ahuyentan el hervor ponzoñoso de los malos espíritus.

La Ruda-hembra, flor de botánica,
aparragada en las huertas indianas
es hijastra de la flora silvestre sin registro official,
sin afinamiento físico ni metafísico.

o sea, yo.

Rue
(Ruta graveoleus)

Rue combats the knotting of nerves,
emptiness of the soul and emptiness of the stomach,
but, above all, its burnt leaves
frighten away the poisonous fervor of evil spirits.

The female rue, botanical flower,
crouched in Spanish-American gardens
is the stepdaughter of wild flora without official record,
without physical or metaphysical refinement

that is, I.

NOTES ON THE POEMS

Page 29: Caupolicán was a Mapuche chief and a leader of the Indian resistance to the Spanish invaders of Chile.

Page 55: Francisco Coloane (1910–2002) Chilean author of novels and short fiction.

Page 63: Malte refers to Malte Laurids Brigge from Rilke's *The Notebooks of Malte Laurids Brigge*. In the book, Malte's grandfather, Christoph Detlev Brigge, dies over a period of several months at the family estate in Ulsgaard.

Page 69: Swedish Nobel Prize winner Selma Lagerlöf (1858–1940) is one of the most famous children's authors in the world. Her classic book *The Wonderful Adventures of Nils Holgersson*, is the story of a Swedish boy who flies off on the wings of a goose.

Page 71: Rahue Alto is a section of the city of Osorno,which is situated at the confluence of the Damas and Rahue Rivers

Page 87: A tucuquere is the Magellanic horned owl.

Page 91: Gustav Mahler (1860–1911) was a Bohemian-Austrian composer and conductor remembered mainly for his symphonies and his symphonic song cycle, *Das Lied von der Erde* (The Song of the Earth).

Page 92: Richard Strauss (1864–1949) was a German composer of the late Romantic era, particularly noted for his tone poems and operas. Franz Lehár (1870–1948) was an Austro-Hungarian composer known mainly for his operettas. "The Waves of the Danube" is a waltz written by Romanian composer Iosef Ivanovici (1845–1902).

Page 93: A kermess is an outdoor fair, often held as a fund-raising event.

Page 95: Johann Wolfgang von Goethe (1749–1832) was a German novelist, dramatist, humanist, scientist, and philosopher best known for his writings about Dr. Faustus.

Page 99: An oxheart cabbage is a pointed head variety of cabbage.

page 103: Ludwig van Beethoven (1770–1827) German composer. His

Symphony No. 6, Op. 68 is the "Pastoral, which conjures up his feelings about the countryside he loved.

Paloma Picasso(1949-) A designer and business woman, she is the daughter of Pablo Picasso.

Page 113: The Huilliche are a group of people indigenous to Southern Chile.

Page 119: Benjamin Subercaseaux (1902–1973) A Chilean writer and poet, he received Chile's National Literature Prize in 1963.

Page 123: Johan Sibelius (1865–1957) Finnish composer and violinist, best-known for *Finlandia* (1899). Knut Hamsun (1859–1952) Norwegian writer who won the Nobel Prize in Literature in 1920 for his novel *Growth of the Soil.* Pablo Neruda (Neftalí Ricardo Reyes Basoalto) (1904–1973) Chilean poet and diplomat, he won the Nobel Prize for literature in 1971 "for a poetry that with the action of an elemental force brings alive a continent's destiny and dreams." Francisco Coloane (1910–2002) Chilean author of novels and short fiction. The Yagán were a tribe native to Chile and now extinct.

Page 127: María Luisa Bombal (1910-1980) was a Chilean novelist and story writer, one of the first to break away from the realistic tradition in Latin America. Jorge Luis Borges (1899–1986) was an Argentine poet, essayist, and short-story writer whose tales of fantasy and dreamworlds are classics of 20th century world literature.

Page 129: Andre Breton (1896–1966) French Surrealist writer. Vicente Huidobro (1893–1948) Chilean poet.

Page 131: Sigmund Freud (1856–1939) was an Austrian phychiatrist and the founder of the psychoanalytic school of psychology. Rainer Maria Rilke (1875–1926) is generally considered to be the German language's greatest poet of the 20th century.

Page 137: Tony Caluga (Abraham Lillo Machuca, 1917–1997) was a famed circus clown.

Page 143: Juan Rulfo (1917–1986) was a Mexican novelist, short story writer, and photographer and one of Latin America's most esteemed writers. In his most famous book, *Pedro Páramo*, Juan Preciado is told by his dying mother to go to the town of Comala to seek his father, Pedro Páramo. Once he arrives there, it's slowly revealed to him that all the residents of Comala are ghosts. Tacamó is the section of Osorno where Delia Dominguez lives.

Page 159: Gabriela refers to Gabriela Mistral (1889-1957), pseudonym for Lucila Godoy y Alcayaga, famed Chilean poet and winner of the Nobel Prize in Literature "for her lyric poetry which, inspired by powerful emotions, has made her name a symbol of the idealistic aspirations of the entire Latin American world."

Page 163: Cumbia: Music and dance typical of the Caribbean coast of Colombia.

Page 165: Rita Hayworth (1918–1987) American film actress; St. Rita of Casia (1381–1457) is known as the Saint of Impossible Things. Tres Medallas is a brand of Chilean wine from a winery in Santa Rita.

Page 171: Isabel appears in Colombian novelist Gabriel Gárcia Márquez's (1928–) book of stories, *Leaf Storm* (first published in 1955) in a story titled "Monologue of Isabel Watching It Rain in Macondo." Mocando is the fictional town that appears in various works by this Nobel Prize-winning author. In the story, Macondo is drenched by rain and emits a palpable odor of decay.

Page 175: Bertolt Brecht (1898–1956) was an influential German dramatist, stage director, and poet. *Mother Courage and Her Children* (1939) is one of his best-known plays. "Clavel del Aire" is an air plant found in Latin America, frequently on branches of aged carob trees or on bare rocky crags.

Page 181: Frida Kahlo (1907–1954) was a Mexican painter. "The Broken Column" (1944) is one of her most famous self-portraits.

Page 195: the Yaganes are the indigenous people of Chile's Magallanes Province.

Page 197: Butahuillimapu means "distant southern lands" in Mapudungun. Icoquih: Venus, the precursor of the sun, literally, "who carries the sun on her back." The *Popul Vuh* (The Book of Council) is a sacred ancient Mayan text considered the bible of the Mayan people.

About the Translators

Roberta Gordenstein has published numerous articles and reviews about Jewish and Latina writers. Her most recent translations have appeared in *The House of Memory* and *Miriam's Daughters*, edited by Marjorie Agosín. Besides her work in literary criticism and translation, she has conducted teacher-training workshops in Eastern Europe and Central America. She is associate professor of Spanish at Elms College in Chicopee, Massachusetts.

Marjorie Agosín is well-known as poet, writer, critic, and human rights activist. Editor of White Pine Press' acclaimed Secret Weavers Series: Writing by Latin American Women, she is a professor at Wellesley College in Massachusetts. Her published titles include *Ashes of Revolt, Happpiness, A Cross and A Star: Memoirs of a Jewish Girl in Chile, Melodious Women, Women in Disguise,* and *Dear Anne Frank.*

The Secret Weavers Series

Woman Without Background Music
SELECTED POEMS OF DELIA DOMINGUEZ.

With Eyes and Soul: Images of Cuba
POEMS BY NANCY MOREJON

I Have Forgotten Your Name
A NOVEL BY MARTHA RIVERA

Open Your Eyes and Soar
CUBAN WOMEN WRITING NOW

A Woman in Her Garden
SELECTED POEMS OF DULCE MARÍA LOYNAZ

Gabriela Mistral: Recados on Women

River of Sorrows
A NOVEL BY LIBERTAD DEMITRÓPULOS

A Secret Weavers Anthology
A SELECTION FROM ALL PREVIOUS VOLUMES IN THE SERIES

A Necklace of Words
WRITING BY MEXICAN WOMEN

What is Secret
STORIES BY CHILEAN WOMEN

These Are Not Sweet Girls
POETRY BY LATIN AMERICAN WOMEN.

Pleasure in the Word
EROTIC WRITING BY LATIN AMERICAN WOMEN

A Gabriela Mistral Reader
A SELECTION OF PROSE AND POETRY

Landscapes of a New Land
FICTION BY LATIN AMERICAN WOMEN

Alfonsina Storni: Selected Poems